SANSKRIT BUDDHISM IN BURMA

PUBLISHER'S NOTE

It might look indeed retrogressive to bring out another reprint of the book originally published in 1936. The present edition has been thoroughly recomposed in its original format with the main objective of providing a better printed and attractive text. Quite understandably a lot of further research must have taken place during the succeeding years.

Since this book still maintains its highly authoritative and reference value, the present venture is to make it available, as a ready reference, to the reading public, especially to scholars and research students.

SANSKRIT BUDDHISM IN BURMA

Nihar Ranjan Ray

M.A. (Cal.) Dr. Litt. & Phil. (Leiden), Dip. Lib. (Lond.)

Mrinalini Gold-Medalist, Griffith Prize-man

Premchand Roychand Scholar

Lecturer in Ancient Indian History & Culture

University of Calcutta

Kaveri Books

New Delhi - 110002

Edition : 2019
ISBN : 978-81-7479-220-4

Published by
Kaveri Books
4832/24, Ansari Road, Daryaganj,
New Delhi - 110 002 (India)
Ph. : 011-2328 8140, 2324 5799
E-mail : kaveribooks@vsnl.com
kaveribooks@gmail.com
Website : www.kaveribooks.com

Typesetting at Creative Graphics, Delhi

PRINTED IN INDIA

To

DR. BIMALA CHURN LAW

M.A., B.L., Ph.D.

as a token of

admiration and gratitude

Acknowledgements

It is my most pleasant duty to record here my deepest feeling of regard and gratitude to Prof. Dr. J. Ph. Vogel who as my promoter took pains to go through the entire manuscript with scrupulous care, suggesting improvements, and always favouring me with his wide knowledge and experience. He did much more than this: he threw the doors of the Kern Institute open to me for my studies; he did all that he could to make my five months' stay in Leiden profitable; and, most of all, it was through his kind efforts and by virtue of his recommendations that the Ministry of Education of the Government of Netherlands gave me special leave to go in for the highest academic distinction of the University of Leiden in so short a time. To him, and also to Mrs. Vogel, I take this opportunity to offer my sincere thanks and gratitude.

I owe my stay in Europe for about a year and a half to the kind and affectionate patronage of Mr. Syamaprasad Mookerjee, M.A., B.L., Barrister-at-Law, who as Vice-Chancellor, and President of the Council of Post-graduate Teaching in Arts, University of Calcutta, made it possible for me to enjoy special study leave privilege that enabled, among other things, the preparation of this humble work. Even in the midst of his heavy duties he has always cared to keep himself in touch with the work I have been doing in Europe; his words of encouragement and his affectionate concern for success in my endeavours have been a source of strength and inspiration to me. My feeling of regard, loyalty and gratitude towards him are too deep for words; and I cannot do more than merely record my indebtedness to him.

This monograph owes its publication in its present form to the generosity of Dr. Bimala Churn Law, M.A., B.L., Ph.D., who is widely known in India and Europe for his valuable contributions to the study of Pāli literature and Buddhism as well as for his kind patronage of scholarship. To him I dedicate this humble piece of work as a token of admiration and gratitude.

It is my duty and pleasure to thank my friend Miss Jessy Blom for kindly preparing the Index.

I must also acknowledge the courtesy of the Archaeological Survey of Burma in kindly extending me permission to publish the illustrations that accompany this monograph.

NIHARRANJAN RAY

December 10, 1936. Kern Institute, Leiden

Preface

This monograph, like my earlier one on *Brahmanical Gods in Burma* (Calcutta University, 1932), attempts to explain one of the many aspects of the culture-complex of early Indo-Burmese history; at the same time it seeks to initiate another chapter in the history of the expansion of Indian religions and culture outside India's natural geographical boundaries. It was originally conceived as a part of a more comprehensive work on the *History of Buddhism in Burma: From the earliest times to the British conquest*, mainly from the historical point of view; but the importance of the subject, as subsequently it appeared to me, justified an independent treatment, and when Prof. Dr. J. Ph. Vogel, Professor of Sanskrit and Indian Archaeology in the University of Leiden, approved of my choice, I decided to present it as a dissertation for the Degree of Doctor in Letters and Philosophy of the University of Leiden which with the now well-known Kern Institute as an adjunct has developed into an important centre of Oriental study and research. The following pages embody the results of my researches in this particular subject.

The title of the dissertation, *Sanskrit Buddhism in Burma*, requires a word of explanation. *Mahāyāna Buddhism in Burma* was out of the question, as my researches led me to infer that the Sarvāstivāda was also at one time prevalent in Burma, as also Tantrayāna and Mantrayāna. The choice lay therefore between adopting either *Northern Buddhism* . . . or *Sanskrit Buddhism* . . .; but as Northern Buddhism is an expression to which exception has often rightly been taken by scholars, I adopted the latter, to indicate nothing more than those forms of Buddhism whose canons are supposed to have been written and preserved in Sanskrit. It is just a convenient title, and nothing more.

The subject of this dissertation is but little known, and very little has so far been done to elucidate the vague general ideas that exist to-day amongst scholars about it. The most important contribution was made by M. Charles Duroiselle in his admirable article on "The Aris of Burma and Tantrik Buddhism" in the *An. R.A.S.I.*, 1915-16; but his work has not yet been followed up except in some meagre and stray notices in the *J.B.R.S.*, the *An. R.A.S.I.*, and the *An. R.A.S.B.* which have been referred to in their proper places in the body of this monograph. No apology is therefore needed, I hope, when I venture to present the subject in the form of a short treatise; but it must be considered as nothing more than a beginning in the study of a subject which requires further elucidation; and I am almost certain that further archaeological research especially with regard to the wall-paintings of Pagan from their iconographic standpoint, and the examination of the contents of old monastic libraries in Upper Burma, will add to our knowledge of the subject.

The materials used in preparing this monograph are mostly archaeological, but it will be seen that I have also drawn from literary sources, but only so far as they are substantiated by archaeological evidence so as to cover all relevant inscriptions, sculptures, paintings and monuments known up to date from Burma. While a fair number of them have already been published in the Reports of the Archaeological Surveys of India and Burma, there has been incorporated information from a large number of sources that are here brought to light for the first time. Apart from new materials that are now made known, there will be found many instances where new interpretations of old materials have been put forward. Thus, I have been led to infer the prevalence of the Sarvāstivāda in Old Prome, the definite existence of Mahāyānist and Tantric texts in the monastic libraries of Upper Burma, and of hitherto unrecognized representations of gods and goddesses belonging to the Mahāyāna and its allied pantheons. I have also been able, I hope, to establish the identity of the Samaṇakuṭṭakas with the Aris, both branded as heterodox sects; to indicate the time when and place whence the Mahḍydna and its allied cults penetrated Burma, and the fact of their existence for a long time even after the glorious reformation of Anawrahta in 1057-1058 A.D. I have also given sufficient indications of the part played by the followers of these cults, whose number must have been considerable at one time, in the religious life of Upper Burma. Some of the identifications of gods and goddesses may be held as doubtful - the identification marks and attributes in a number of instances are either absent or indistinct-, but the major conclusions based on them and on other materials, equally important, are expected to endure. These conclusions have been summarised in the final chapter.

Kern Institute, Leiden **Niharranjan Ray**

December 10, 1936

Abbreviations

A.O.	Acta Orientalia (Leiden).
An. R.A.S.B.	Annual Report of the Archaeological Survey of Burma (Rangoon).
An. R.A.S.I.	Annual Report of the Archaeological Survey of India (Simla and Delhi).
B.E.F.E.O.	Bulletin de l'Ecole Française d'Extrême-Orient (Hanoi).
Cal. Rev.	The Calcutta Review (Calcutta).
Ep. Birim.	Epigraphia Birminica (Rangoon).
Ep. Ind.	Epigraphia Indica (Simla and Delhi).
Ind. Ast.	Indian Antiquary (Bombay).
Ind. Hist. Quart.	The Indian Historical Quarterly (Calcutta).
J.A.	Journal Asiatique (Paris).
J.A.S.B.	Journal of the Asiatic Society of Bengal (Calcutta).
J.B.R.S.	Journal of the Burma Research Society (Rangoon).
J.I.S.O.A.	Journal of the Indian Society of Oriental Art (Calcutta).
P.T.S.	Pali Text Society (London).

Other abbreviations are easily intelligible

Contents

Acknowledgements vii

Preface ix

Abbreviations xiii

Introduction 1

1. Sarvāstivāda in Ancient Prome 19
2. Sanskrit Inscriptions: Sanskrit Buddhist Texts 31
3. Gods and Goddesses of Northern Buddhism 40
4. The Ari Sect and the Samaṇakuṭṭakas: Tantric Buddhism in Burma 62
5. Testimony of Buddhist Monks 72
6. When and Whence did Sanskrit Buddhism Penetrate Burma? 88

Conclusions 96

Bibliography 100

Index 102

Description of Plates 112

Plates 117

Introduction

As seen on the map of Asia, Burma looks as if it were an outstretched hand of the Indian continent rather than a part of the South-East-Asiatic countries bordering the Indian Ocean, which collectively we know as Further India. Indeed, ethnologically and linguistically, and also geographically, Burma is more a component part of the whole area now covered by Burma, Siam, Indo-China and the Malay Peninsula, than of India proper to whose cultural influence she, like the rest of the countries of Indo-China, submitted herself for centuries. But notwithstanding that strong cultural domination by India, mainly exerted through the all-pervading faith of Theravada Buddhism, Burma maintained from the very beginning of her history a distinct political, social, and even cultural character. Unlike Ceylon, Burma hardly ever merged herself into the currents and cross-currents of Indian historical and cultural evolution, and it is only with the British conquest and consequent unification of Burma with the Indian empire, evidently for administrative convenience, that the country came within the domain of practical Indian life and politics. Otherwise, there is no historical reason why Burma should be considered, as it is so often done, as a part of India. Her history runs a parallel course, so far as relations with India are concerned, with that of the other countries of Further India, and the islands of the Malay Archipelago, collectively known to historians as Indonesia. The Indo-Burmese chapter of the history of Burma can be understood in its proper perspective and real significance only when we take this vital historical fact into account. It is also a key to a better understanding of the history of Indian cultural influence in Burma.

Burma Professes the Buddhism of the Theravāda School

Like Siam, Burma till to-day is professedly Buddhist, following the Pāli canon of the Southern School. Nowhere else in the countries and islands once won over to Indian cultural enterprise is Indianism to-day a living and regulating factor of any importance[1]; and nowhere an Indian faith is of deeper significance, or wields a stronger influence in the socio-political life of the people than Buddhism does in Burma. Indeed, Burma owes her spiritual and cultural existence to the undying appeal of Theravāda Buddhism which has remained the chief factor in the life and character of the average Burman as of the entire Burmese nation.

The story of the introduction of Buddhism in Pagan in Upper Burma, repeated again and again in Pāli and Burmese chronicles and Mon inscriptions of Burma[2], is much too well-known to need any description here. Suffice it to say that it was introduced from Thaton, the Talaing capital of Lower Burma, known in ancient days as Ramaññadesa, the land *par excellence* of the Talaings, while Upper Burma was known as Mrammadesa, the land *par excellence* of the Burmese. This historic event took place in the third quarter of the eleventh century of the Christian era, in 1057, Or, perhaps, 1058, to be more exact, when Pagan was fast rising to importance.

At the end of a long siege Thaton ceased to be a royal capital, and Anawrahta (1044-1077), the victorious king of Pagan, returned to his capital with the most valuable treasures of the faith, nearly the entire host of monks, and with them thirty-two white elephants, each laden with scriptures and relics, all belonging to Manuha, the Talaing king of Thaton. Thaton was annexed and Manuha kept for the rest of his life a captive at Myinpagan, a suburban village near Pagan, while his scriptural treasures were housed in the Bidagataik (Tripiṭaka library), the library building standing to this day not very far from the famous Ānanda Temple. The host of captive monks were released and pushed into the service of propagating the religion of Śākyamuni far and wide in the realm of the new dynasty

1. Except perhaps in Bali where Brahmanism wields a strong influence even to-day, and where one can also detect some faint traces of Buddhism.
2. For example, the *Sāsamavaṁsa*, the *Hmannan Yazawin*, the most important Burmese chronicle, and the long Kalyāṇi Inscriptions of King Dhammaceti of Pegu (*Ep. Birm.* III, ii.).
See also my *Brahmanical Gods in Burma*, Calcutta University, 1932, pp. I-2. Also my work on *History of Buddhism in Burma*, chap. I.

of kings. Thus, once again the superior culture of the vanquished predominated over that of the victors, and the Southern Buddhism of Lower Burma gradually spread throughout Upper Burma till it embraced, after various vicissitudes of fortune, the whole country under one religious organisation. From the eleventh century onwards, Burma has never wavered from her faith in Buddhism.

The question now will naturally be asked: When did Thaton receive the faith of Theravāda Buddhism, or more correctly speaking, the Hīnayāna form of Buddhism? Are we to accept the tradition, so insistent in Burmese records, of the Asoka mission of Soṇa and Uttara to Suvaṇṇabhūmi? Shall we also believe the later tradition, equally vocal in Burmese chronicles, of Buddhaghosa's crossing over to Burma and preaching there the religion of the Master?

Available evidence is so meagre that none of these questions can be answered satisfactorily. Recent criticism has thrown doubt on both traditions[1], referred to above, though evidence is daily accumulating in favour of an early introduction of Buddhism in Burma.

All that can be asserted with certainly at this stage of historical research is that the introduction of the faith must have taken place not later than the 6th century, but the actual circumnstances are unknown. The earliest epigraphic records found in Burma hail not from Thaton, but from the small village of Hmawza, six miles north of the modern town of Prome. The village which is scattered over with ancient remains has been identified with the old capital city of the Pyus, the P'iao of the Chinese; indeed it was the heart of the country known to the Chinese as Shih-li-ch'a-ta-lo and to the Burmese as Thārikhittara (Sanskrit: Śrīkṣetra).

The inscriptions referred to consist of two gold plates discovered at Maunggan[2], a small village close to Hmawza; three fragments of a stone inscription[3] found while clearing some *debris* round the base of the Bawbawgyi Pagoda in Hmawza proper; a line of inscription

1. Foulkes, "Buddhaghosa", *Ind. Ant.*, XIX, 1889, p. 122; Smith, "Asoka's alleged mission to Pegu", *Ind. Ant.*, XXXIV, 1905; Hackmann, *Buddhism as a religion,* p. 63; Finot, "The Legend of Buddhaghosa", *Cal. Rev.*, 1923. pp. 63-67.

2. *Ep. Ind.*, V, pp. 101 ff; Finot, "Un nouveau document sur le buddhisme in birman", *J. A.*, Juit-Aout, 1912, p. 121 ff.

3. Finot, *ibid.*; *An. R.A.S.B.*, 1924, p. 22.

around the rim of the lid of a small relic casket, also discovered at Hmawza[1]; a book of twenty leaves of gold, each inscribed on one side in the manner of the old palm-leaf manuscripts of India, placed within two covers of the same metal[2]; and an inscribed gold leaf from the Kyundawza village, also near Hmawza[3]. The language of these inscriptions is Pāli, and, what is more significant, they are all written in a character which is closely akin to the Kānāḍā-Telegu script of Bühler but which Finot prefers to call Kadamba. Paleographically, these epigraphic records cannot be dated far out of the 6th century of the Christian era, if not earlier. But the most interesting fact is that all tliese records contain extracts from well-known Pāli texts like the *Vibhaṅga* and the *Aṅguttara Nikāya*, and one of them, the gold-leaf book, contains, among other things, the *Paticca samuppāda Sutta*, viz., the *sutta* itself with its nirodha but without the *vibhaṅga*[4].

The extracts, however, are not quoted *verbatim*. The evident conclusion to be drawn from these records is that Pali Buddhism was already an established religion at least as early as the 5th or 6th century; that Pāli Buddhism as the language of the Theravāda was known and understood in ancient Prome by at least a section of the people; that Pali canonical texts were studied in their doctrinal aspects; and finally, what is most important, that the original home from where this Pāli Buddhism was introduced in Lower Burma was evidently the Andhra-Pallava region of South India, from such centres as Amarāvatī, Nāgārjunīkoṇḍa, Kāñcīpuram, Kāverīpattanam and Uragapuram where Theravāda Buddhism during these centuries had established famous and flourishing strongholds, and which places, particularly the last three, are intimately associated with the Buddhaghosa tradition[5].

---

1. *An. R.A.S.I.*, 1926-27, pp. 172-73
2. *An. R.A.S.I.*, 1926-27, p. 200.
3. *An, R.A.S.I.*, 1928-29, p. 109.
4. These records have been fully analysed and discussed in all their bearings in the first chapter of my forthcoming volume on *History of Buddhism in Burma: from the earliest times to the British conquest*. There will be found an attempt to reconstruct the early history of Theravāda Buddhism in Burma, and its later vicissitudes after the introduction of the religion into Pagan in A.D. 1057, down to 1824.
5. These findings tend to point to the conclusion that "Theravāda Buddhism which in Burma to-day is of the Ceylonese form was originally introduced

Earliest Contacts of Burma with India : Evidence of Archaeology

It should incidentally be mentioned that these epigraphic records, besides being the earliest evidences of the introduction of Buddhism in Burma, are also the earliest documents of the history of Indo-Burmese relations. It is also worth mentioning that the earliest documents of Brahmanism in Lower Burma, from Old Prome, images of Brahmanical gods and goddesses stylistically dateable in about the seventh century, owe their inspiration to the Veṅgī-Pallava art tradition, and those from Thaton, belonging to about the ninth and tenth centuries, seem to be affiliated to the Orissan tradition of sculpture[1]. In any case, available evidence at our disposal tends to show that during the early centuries the current of Indian colonial enterprise in Lower Burma flowed mainly from the eastern coastal regions of South India, extending from ancient Kalinga down to the Cola country.

Indian Expansion in Indo-China and Indonesia: Epigraphic Documents

A rapid parallel survey of Indian projection into the countries of Indo-China and the islands of Indonesia also brings out the same

---

not from Ceylon, but from South India, where in the time of I-tsing (671-95), all followed the Sthavira-nikāya though there existed a few adherents of other nikāyas also" (Takakusu, *I-tsing's Records of the Buddhist Religion,* pp. xxiii-xxiv). In fact it was not till the middle of the twelfth century that Ceylon came to play any important role in the history of Buddhism in : Burma. It was in 1167 when Panthagu, the then primate of the kingdom chose Ceylon as the place of self-banishment in consequence of his repugnance at the conduct of the then reigning king of Pagan, and in 1180 when Uttarajiva the primate who had succeeded Pantbagu, returned from a pilgrimage to Ceylon as the "First Pilgrim of Ceylon" that the island came to acquire a holy sanctity in the eyes of the Burmese followers of the faith. In 1190, Capata, Uttarajiva's disciple, earned the title of "Second Pilgrim of Ceylon" and on his return tried to convert the whole realm to the Ceylonese form. These missions and intercourses coupled with Capata's attempts to Ceylonize Burmese Buddhism led to the gradual prodominance of Ceylonese Buddhism in Burma and the wiping out of even the memory of the original source. Moreover, the centre of Theravāda Buddhism had also by that time been shifted from South India to Ceylon". See my *History of Buddhism in Burma... op. cit.*, chap. I.

1. See my *Brahmanical Gods in Burma*, pp. 75-79, plates II and V.

historical fact, though the source of inspiration is now mainly centred in the realm of the Pallavas, which extended, in the seventh and eighth centuries, all over the south-eastern coast from the Godāvarī region down to at least the Kāverī. All the epigraphic records, some dated and the rest dateable on paleographical grounds from c. 400 A.D. to about the middle of the eighth century, are written in what is known as Pallava-Grantha characters of SouthEastern India[1]. The majority of these records are Brahmanical, but there are quite a number which point to the prevalence of Buddhism during these centuries in the islands and countries of the South-Eastern seas. Thus the inscription of the mahānāvika Buddhagupta, found near the ruins of an old Buddhist temple in the Wellesley Province of the Malay Peninsula is a Buddhist document, paleographically dateable in the 5th century, as perhaps also the Kedah inscription (found at Kedah near Bukit Muriam) of still earlier date. The Talang Tuwo inscription of Sumatra, discovered not very far from modern Palembang, and dated in the Śaka year 606 (684 A.D.), is a religious document, and if the terms occurring in it are any indication, it is Buddhistic (compare such terms as *vo[bo]dhicitta, ratnatraya, vajraśarīra, asuttarābhisamyaksamvo* [*bo*]*dhi,* etc.)[2].

From West Borneo we have a series of as many as eight short Sanskrit epigraphs, paleographically dateable in the fifth century which definitely testify to the existence of Buddhism in that part of the island at that early period[3]. One of the earliest inscriptions of the ancient kingdom of Fou-nan, discovered at the monument of Tā Prohm in the province of Bāti, and dateable paleographically and with the help of the Chinese texts at the disposal of M. Pelliot, in about the first quarter of the seventh century, is also frankly a Buddhist document. It states, among other things, that Buddha, Dharma and Sangha are in a flourishing condition; and though the purport of the inscription is not clear, it can be surmised that it

---

1. For a revised and latest study of these inscriptions, see, *Expansion of Indo-Aryan culture during Pallava rule as evidenced by inscriptions*, by B. Ch. Chhabra, in *J.A.S.B., Letters*, Vol. I, 1935, no. 1, pp. 14-55.
2. *B.E.F.E.O.*, XXX, pp. 29-80; A.O., II, p. 12; Chhabra, *op. cit.*, pp. 29-30.
3. *An. R.A.S.I.*, 1910-11, pp. 40 ff; Chhabra, *op. cit.*, p. 41 ff; Vogel, *Bijdragen*, LXXIV, 1918, pp. 167-132, LXXVI; pp. 431-434.

recorded the foundation of a Buddhist sanctuary[1]. This inscription studied along with other early inscriptions of Kamboja, particularly with the Viṣṇuite inscription of Prince Guṇavarman, found among the ruins of the monuments of Pràsàt Pràm Lovên on the hill of Thap-muòi[2], reveals the interesting fact that in contemporary Kamboja as in Borneo, Brahmanism and Buddhism existed side by side. It is significant that in Burma, too, during the early centuries of definite Indian contacts, a similar state of affairs is equally noticeable; no less important is also the fact that, as in Kamboja, so in Burma, the prevailing cult of Brahmanism was that of Viṣṇu[3]. Another early dated inscription of Kamboja (Śaka year 586=664 A.D.), the Vat Prey Vier Sanskrit inscription, is also definitely a Buddhist record, speaking of two bhikṣus, Ratnabhānu and Ratnasiṁha, who were born of the same mother *(sodarau)*[4]. That in Kamboja, Buddhism flourished already in the later half of the fifth century A.D. is also attested to by Chinese texts which have yielded to M. Pelliot the important information that in 484 A.D. Jayavarman (king of Fou-nan, who is also referred to in the inscription discovered at Tā Prohm, cited above) sent the Indian monk Śākya Nāgasena to present a memorial in the Chinese Imperial court which began with a panegyric of the Emperor as one of the patrons of Buddhism, in whose empire the Law flourished more and more[5].

Relative Position of The Different Schools of Buddhism in Further India and Indonesia

Sarvāstivāda

It is difficult to ascertain to which school this early Buddhism of the Hinduised countries of the South-Eastern seas owed its origin. It is possible that the Hīnayāna of the Sthaviravāda school may have preceded the Sarvāstivāda and the Mahāyāna, but there is no definite evidence to help us in our assumption. If the language (Sanskrit) of the inscriptions of the Malay Peninsula, West-Borneo

1. Coedès, *B.E.F.E.O.*, XXXI, pp. 1-12.
2. Coedès, *ibid.*
3. See my *Brahmanical Gods...*, pp. 15-49.
4. Bergaigne, *Inscriptions...*, pp. 61-62; Chatterji, *Indian cultural influence in Cambodia*, p. 55.
5. Chatterji, *Indian cultural influence in Cambodia*, p. 22.

and Kamboja is any indication of the school, it may be inferred that the Buddhism we catch a glimpse of in them is of the Sarvāstivāda form. This inference gains strength from what we all know from Chinese sources about the state of religion in these islands and countries in the seventh century of the Christian era. When Fa-hien visited Java (from Ceylon) in about 412 A.D., there were many Brahmins in the island, and Buddhism was practically of no importance. In fact, Java was mostly given up to Brahmanism till it came under the political and cultural domination of the Sumatran empire of Śrīvijaya. However, in other islands and countries of the region, so far as definite available evidence goes, Buddhism began to assert itself not earlier than the middle of the fifth century, so that when I-tsing, towards the close of the seventh century wrote his celebrated *Records of the Buddhist Religion*, based on extensive travels in India, Ceylon and the Indian Archipelago, he found that in the islands of the Southern Sea, consisting of more than ten countries, the Mūlasarvāstivāda-nikāya had been universally adopted, exept in Malayu (Śrī Bhoja = Śrīvijaya = Sumatra) where there were a few who belonged to the Mahāyāna[1]. And on this point I-tsing certainly could not mis-state facts, for he himself subscribed to the school of the Sarvāstivāda.

Here then is the first problem before us. We know definitely that the Theravāda was prevalent in Burma from about the 5th century. But is it likely that the Sarvāstivāda was also known and practised in Burma in about the time I-tsing speaks of? Does I-tsing include any part of Burma when he speaks of the countries of the Southern Sea? Or, else, is there any other independent evidence of the existence of Sarvāstivāda Buddhism in Burma? This is one of the first questions that we have to answer. If it had existed in Lin-i (= Campa) where the Buddhists generally belonged to the Āryasammiti-nikāya, though there were also a few followers of the Sarvāstīvāda-nikāya[2], as well as in She-ho-po-ti (= Dvāravati near Ayuthia in Siam), and I-tsing seems to suggest that it did, there is all likelihood that Burma, a close neighbour of these two countries, did not remain untouched by this wave of the Sarvāstivāda.

1. Takakusu, *I-tsing's Records of the Buddhist Religion.*

2. Takakusu, *op. cit.*, p. 12.

Mahāyāna

The gradual ascendancy of Śrīvijaya of Sumatra to the status of an imperial power, exercising sovereignty over the neighbouring islands of the Archipelago from the third quarter of the seventh century, introduces a new culture-complex into the early history of Indo-China and Indonesia. The earliest inscriptions of this new power, discovered in Sumatra, and three of them dated in Śaka years 605, 606 and 608 (683, 684 and 686 A.D.), are all written in what is now known as Old Malay, interspersed with a large number of Sanskrit words[1]. One of these, the Talang Tuwo inscription (684 A.D.) referred to above, has a number of Sanskrit words that seem to point to the Mahāyāna form of Buddhism. This is perfectly in accord with what I-tsing has to say about the Buddhism of Malayu (= Śrī Bhoja = Śrīvijaya) of almost exactly the same time[2]. By the middle of the eighth century, the Śailendra kings of Śrīvijaya had already come into the possession not only of the Malay Peninsula but also of Java and the neighbouring islands. The earliest dated Śailendra record from the Malay Peninsula hails from Ligor[3]. It is written in Sanskrit, and records the erection of three brick temples dedicated by a Śailendra king to the Śākyamuni and his two associates, Padmapāṇi and Vajrapāṇi. The inscription is dated in the Śaka year 697 which corresponds to 775 A.D. [4]. The earliest dated Śailendra inscription from Java is also a Mahāyāna document. It is the celebrated Kalasan inscription, dated in the Śaka year 700 (= 778 A.D.), which records the erection of a temple dedicated to the goddess Tārā, at the instance of the Śailendra king of Śrivijaya. The temple of Kalasan which stands to this day not very far from the magnificent Barabudur, is certainly that temple of Tārā referred to in the inscription. Following the Kalasan record comes another inscription, found at Kelurak and dated in the Śaka year 704 (= 782 A.D.), which refers to the consecration of an image of the Bodhisattva Mañjuśrī or Mañjughoṣa at the instance of the

1. Coedés, *B.E.F.E.O.*, XXX, pp. 29-80.
2. Takakusu, *op. cit.*
3. *Bijdragen*, 83, p. 462, f.n.; Krom, *Hindoe-Jav. Geschiedenis,* 2nd edn. p. 130; Chhabra, *op. cit.*, pp. 20-27; Chatterji and Chakravarti, *India and Java,* Greater India Society, Calcutta, pp. 40-44.
4. Chhabra, *op. cit.*, p. 22.

guru of a king who is described as the "ornament of the Śailendra dynasty". The Nālandā copper-plate of Devapāla of Bengal (last quarter of the 9th century) granting some villages for the upkeep of the monastery built at Nālandā, the celebrated seat of the Mahāyānist university, by Bālaputradeva of the Śailendra dynasty, and the Cola inscription (first quarter of the eleventh century) commemorating the gift of a village to a Buddhist vihāra at Negapatam, built by another king of the Śailendra dynasty, also reveal the fervent zeal and ardour of the kings of Śrivijaya in the cause of Mahāyāna Buddhism. A Nepalese manuscript of the elventh century containing miniature paintings of important Mahāyāna images at well-known centres of Buddhism, has one painting representing Lokanātha at Śrīvijayapura in Suvarṇapura (Sumatra)[1]. This Śrīvijaya, reputed as a stronghold of Mahāyāna Buddhism, attracted the celebrated Bengali Buddhist monk Atīśa (980-1053) in the eleventh century, who went there to consult a learned Buddhist monk in that distant island[2]. And it is to the Śailendra dynasty of Śrīvijaya that we owe the beautiful series of Mahāyānist temples now represented by the Caṇḍī Kalasan, the Caṇḍī Pawon and the Caṇḍi Mĕndut, and perhaps also the magnificent Barabuḍur.

The zeal of the Śailendras for the cause of the Mahāyāna did not leave the neighbouring countries of Indo-China untouched and uninfluenced. It was probably under the aegis of this dynasty that the Mahāyāna spread to the Malay Peninsula which presumably was embraced within the Śrīvijaya empire till at least as late as the eleventh century. In the Cambridge MS. referred to above we have two miniatures, one inscribed: *Kahtāhadvīpe* (Katāha = Kheda) *Valavatīparvate Lokanātha dvādaśa parivartta ārisa,* and another: *Kahtāhadvīpe Valavatīparvate-Lokanātha.* Both of them perhaps refer to the same temple which presumably was dedicated to the Mahāyāna god Lokanātha[3]. Dr. B. R. Chatterji has shown in his

1. Camb. MS. no. Add. 1643. *Suvarṇapure Srivijayapure Lokanātha āriṣasthāna* (fol. 99, V°. I, p. 105). Compare also in this connection, another miniature inscribed: *Yavadvīpe Dīpaṅkara(ḥ),* in Camb. MS. no. Add. 1643. fol. 2, v°. p. 79; A.S.B. MS. no. A 15, fol. 83 r°., p. 79.
2. S. C. Das, *Indian Pandits in the Land of Snow.*
3. Camb. MS. no. Add. 1643, fol. 120 a, v°, 2, p. 102; *ibid,* fol. 120 b, r°. 2, p. 102,

Indian Cultural Influence in Cambodia, that the Śailendras of Śrivijaya, towards the end of the eighth and the beginning of the ninth centuries, exercised some sort of suzerainty over Kamboja; a naval raid by Śrivijaya on the capital of Kamboja is actually recorded, and it is held that the Kamboja king Jayavarman II (802-869) had been to Java (which is said to have included both Sumatra and Java) for some time. After his return to his own country Jayavarman built three capitals in succession: Hariharālaya, Amarendrapura and Mahendraparvata. Amarendrapura, identified with Banteai Chmar, has been found to be essentially a Mahāyānist city presided over by Avalokiteśvara[1]. M. Finot believed[2] that even Angkor Thom which is known to have been a Śaiva city founded by the fervent Śaiva Yaśovarman began in reality as a Buddhist city founded by Jayavarman II. Recent discoveries at the ruins of city have yielded images of the Mahāyāna god Lokeśvara on the gates of the city, and in the temple of Bayon itself an Avalokiteśvara image has been found. Between Angkor Thom and Banteai Chmar many vestiges of the Lokeśvara cult have been discovered; but all these representations of Mahāyānist divinities show signs of ruthless mutiliation, evidently by later Śivaites. Dr. Chatterji suggests that the Mahāyāna came with Jayavarman II from Śrivijaya[3]. Howsoever one may doubt[4] if Jayavarman really returned a Buddhist from Java, or whether Angkor Thom began as a Buddhist city, there can be no doubt about the existence of the Mahāyāna in the capital city of Kamboja in about the ninth century. The images of Mahāyāna deities found from amidst the ruins of the city are positive proofs of that fact. In about the tenth and eleventh centuries Mahāyāna Buddhism seems to have grown more in popularity; for, besides images and inscriptions testifying to the prevalence of the cult[5], we have at least one reference to a temple of Tārā in Kamboja in the Cambridge MS.

1. *B.E.F.E.O.,* XXV, p. 294.
2. *Etudes Asiatiques,* I, pp. 227-256.
3. Chatterji, *op. cit.*
4. Bagchi, P.C., Ind. Hist. *Quart.*, VI, pp. 106-107.
5. King Rājendravarman (944-968) is said to have consecrated several Mahāyāna images. Under his successor, Jayavarman V (968-1001), Mahāyāna Buddhism grew still more in importance.

referred to above. The miniature is inscribed: *Kambojadeśe Tārā(ḥ)*[1], and doubtless refers to a temple dedicated to that goddess.

In Campa, too, Mahāyāna Buddhism flourished already in the ninth century. King Indravarman II (875, 889 A.D.) was a fervent Buddhist, and he was probably the builder of the Mahāyānist Buddhist shrines of Dong Duong dedicated to the god Lokeśvara. Towards the end of the eleventh and in the twelfth century, it gradually grew into importance. Prince Pan became king in 1081 with the title of Parama Bodhisattva, while one of his successors, Jaya Indravarman IV (1163-1170), described himself as a learned scholar of the Mahāyāna and the Dharmaśāstras.

It is a significant fact that all the Sanskrit records which testify to the prevalence of Mahāyāna Buddhism in Further India and Indonesia are written no longer in the Pallava-Grantha character which had been the case till the middle of the eighth century, but in the North Indian Nāgarī character, acording to Dr. Chatterji, in the proto-Bengali character. This, backed by other arguments of historical interrelations between Eastern India and the countries and islands of the Southern Seas, has led Dr. Chatterji and other scholars (e.g., Prof. N. J. Krom) to hold that it was from Bengal and the Magadhan regions that Mahāyāna Buddhism was introduced into the islands of the Archipelago and the countries of Further India[2].

Tantrayāna

Of still more significance is the prevalence of the Tantrayāna in Java, Sumatra and Kamboja, a fact now definitely established by modern researches into the character of Mahāyāna Buddhism and Śivaism in these parts of the Indian Orient. Already in a Kamboja inscription of the ninth century A.D. there is definite evidence of the teaching of Tantric texts at the court of Jayavarman II (802-869). In a Kamboja record of the 11th century there is a reference to the "Tantras of the Paramis"; and images of Hevajra, definitely a Tantric divinity, have been recovered from amidst the ruins of Angkor Thom[3]. A number of Kamboja inscriptions refer to several kings who were initiated into the Great Secret *(Vrah Guhya)* by their

1. Foucher, *Iconographie Bouddhique,* II. p.
2. Chatterji, *op. cit.*, pp. 253 ff; also the same author's *India and Java,* pp. 4-5.
3. A Hevajra image has also been found in Sumatra.

Brahmanical *gurus*; the Śaiva records make obvious references to Tantric doctrines that had crept into Śivaism.

But it was in Java and Sumatra that Tantrayāna seems to have attained greater importance. There Mahāyāna Buddhism and the cult of Śiva, both deeply imbued with Tāntric influence, are to be seen often blending with one another during this period. The Sang *hyang Kamahāyānikan,* consisting of Sanskrit verses explained by an Old Javanese commentary, professes to teach the Mahāyāna and the Mantrayāna. Sir Charles Eliot thinks that it offers many parallels to Nepalese Tantric literature, which, as we know, consists of the teachings of the Buddhist monks of Magadha and Bengal during the Pāla period. According to this treatise, Brahmā, Viṣṇu and Śiva are emanations of the Dhyāni-Buddha Vairocana. The *pañca makāras* are also referred to in this strange work. Another Kawi text, which gives the story of Kuñjarakarṇa, extols Vairocana as being Śiva and Buddha in one[1]. Mr. Moens[2] quotes extracts from Prapañca's panegyric Kawi poem, the *Nāgarakrĕtāgama,* which shows that Krĕtanagara, the ruler of Singasari, was definitely given up to Tantric practices. A statue of this king has been found in a cremation ground which is a certain proof of his profession of Tantric doctrines; in fact the *Nāgarakrĕtāgama* states that Krétanagara had gone through the ten ceremonies of purification and the eight processes of initiation and that he carried out with scrupulons care the five *makāras* 'free from all sensualities'. The inscription engraved on the pedestal of his statue in the robes of a monk records that after his initiation on a cremation ground, he was supposed to be identified with Akṣobhya. The Tantric inscriptions of the Sumatran Prince Ādityavarman (c. 1343-1378 A.D.), dated in the Śaka years 1269 (= 1347) and 1297 (= 1375), also refer in unmistakable language to Tantric practices undergone by the prince and to the evident Tantric character of the Buddhism he seems to have professed[3]. It is again Dr. Chatterji's very able conclusion that this Tantrayāna with its peculiar blending of

1. Chatterji, *op. cit.* pp. 260-261.
2. I. J. L. Moens, *Tijdschrift voor Indische Taal.... Land en Volkenkunde* ..., LXIV, 1924.
3. For details, see, Moens, *op. cit;* also Chatterji, *Indian Cultural Influence* ..., pp. 258-262; India and Java, pp. 52-55.

Śivaism with the Mahāyāna was introduced into Java, Sumatra and Kamboja from Eastern India, now comprised by the modern provinces of Bengal and Bihar, and perhaps also from Nepal and Tibet which were deeply influenced by Pāla Bengal and Bihar[1].

Mahāyāna Buddhism in Burma: A Prima Facie Case

The above rapid survey of the documental background of the history of Mahāyāna and Tantrayāna in Further India and Indonesia has its obvious significance for an understanding of the history of Buddhism in Burma during these centuries. We know that from 1057 A.D., Upper Burma, and within another couple of centuries, also Lower Burma, became definitely committed to Theravāda Buddhism, and even before that period, the prevailing form of religion was the same Theravāda. But did Burma escape altogether this wave of the Mahāyāna and the Tantrayāna that Swept the lands farther south and east and largely influenced the life and culture of the people of the times? Is there not, in Upper Burma, any trace of the Mahāyāna or any other later form of Buddhism that may have crept in before or after the introduction of Theravāda Buddhism into Pagan by Anawrahta in 1057 A.D.? If traces there are, did the cult or cults become extinct after the glorious inauguration of the new religion received from the Talaing country? Is there any trace of Tantric practices or Tantric texts in Burma? Geographically, Burma lies in the midway between Campa and Kamboja, both by land and sea, and she holds the same position, by sea, in relation to Java and Sumatra. It is not unlikely that ships sailing from the East Indian port of Tāmralipti for the islands and countries beyond the Bay, some of them atleast, would touch the ports of Burma and even make them their objective, and drop some of the missionaries along with traders and adventurers, as they certainly did in Java and Sumatra, Campa and Kamboja. With Upper Burma, there was moreover the possibility of a land route through Assam and Manipur; in fact a live land route really existed as late as the eighteenth century along which the Manipuris and Burmese led their respective raids

1. For a detailed acccount of the Buddhism of Barabuḍur in particular and Java in general, see, Krom, *Barabuḍur,* II, the last chapter, on the "Buddhism of Barabuḍur".

into Burma and Manipur[1]. M. Ferrand also recognises the existence of such a route which passed through the Upper Chindwin Valley in Upper Burma, till as late as the seventeenth century (c. 1663 A.D.)[2]. The existence of a land route through Assam and Manipur is also attested to by Burmese chronicles which refer to certain immigrations from North India in a very early period. One of these immigrations is said to have been responsible for the foundation of the city and dynasty of Tagoing on the Irrawady[3], and identified generally with Tugma of Ptolemy. A *prima facie* case lies, therefore, in favour of the possible introduction of Mahāyānist and Tantric influences at least in Upper Burma.

If, therefore, the above questions are answered in the affirmative, further questions will be asked: Which were the circumstances that led to the introduction of this and similar cults of Buddhism? What, again, was the relative position of the Theravāda and Mahāyāna in Burma, and what was the attitude of the people and the ruling authorities? And, how, finally did the Mahāyāna and allied cults influence the Theravāda, if they did at all ?

Present State of Our Knowledge

Before an attempt is made to discuss any of these questions, we have to take a short and rapid survey of the present state of our knowledge about the subject of our study.

Buddhist Sanskrit inscriptions written in North-east Indian Nāgarī characters, discovered at the ruins of ancient Prome and belonging to about the sixth and seventh centuries, have been known for about seven or eight years, and though it has been recognized that they owe their inspiration to a school of Buddhism other than the Theravāda, no attempt has yet been made to interpret their significance in the history of Buddhism in Burma. Later Sanskrit epigraphs, mostly on terracotta votive tablets, in Nāgarī

1. Compare, for example, the raids of the Manipuris on Thaungdut on the Chindwin river in 1647 and 1692, on Myedu in Shwebo in 1735 and 1740; Burmese counter-raids on Manipur in 1755, 1758-59, and even as late as 1813.
2. *Ralations de voyages et Textes geographiques relatifs a l'Extreme Orient,* II, pp. 556-57.
3. *Glass Palace Chronicle,* pp. I-4.

and proto-Bengali characters, and recovered from the ruins of Pagan, have been correctly interpreted by M. Duroiselle to have belonged to the Mahāyāna tradition. The same scholar also proved clearly and unmistakably for the first time[1], that the well-known sect of the Aris of Upper Burma was a Mahāyānist Buddhist sect grossly addicted to Tantric practices; in this connection he also brought out the significance of some of the paintings on the walls of a group of temples of Pagan, notably those of the Paya-thon-zu and Nandamañña. He also suggested that this Tantric character of Buddhism may have been due to contemporary religious influences from Bengal.

Images of gods and goddesses discovered from time to time have also been identified as belonging to the Mahāyāna pantheon, but their significance has been little understood; some of them, and they constitute a good number, have only lately been recognized as Mahāyāna divinities[2]. Some gods of the Mahāyāna pantheon have also been incorporated in the Hīnayāna mythology of Burma, but this curious fusion still remains enexplained.

The existence of a heterodox sect, the Samaṇakuṭṭakas, was also known for a long time; the *Sāsanavaṁsa* refers to them as a strong and powerful sect that acquired a footing in Pagan at a very early period[3]. But no attempt has yet been made to find out who these. Samaṇakuṭṭakas were or what was the significance of the religious tenets and rites they held and practised.

In short, it has been generally recognized that Mahāyāna Buddhism and a baser sort of Mahāyānist Tantrism were known in Upper Burma, but our knowledge does not extend very far in that direction. Our knowledge of the circumstances that led to the introduction of these cults are vague and much too general; nor has any idea been entertained as to the possibility of the prevalence of any other form of Sanskrit Buddhism. No attempt has also been made to evaluate the extent of influence which these different schools of Sanskrit Buddhism gained in Burma,

1. Duroiselle, "The Aris of Burma and Tāntrik Buddhism", in *An. R.A.S.I.*, 1915-16, pp. 79-83.
2. See my article on "The cult of Lokanātha, and other Mahāyāna gods in Burma", in *Buddhistic Studies,* Calcutta, 1931, I.
3. *Sāsanavaṁsa,* P.T.S., pp. 15-17.

or how they reacted on the minds of the people and their religion, the Theravāda. The problem has not also been approached from the Indian side, and the Indian documents, mostly Tibetan, have not been thoroughly analysed so as to yield their fullest information.

Of course, this has been largely due to the Burmese denial of the existence of any other school of Buddhism other than the Theravāda. Indeed, the Burmese people and their mass of old historical literature do not seem to know of any other religion than what they profess to-day and have been doing so for centuries. This silence of authentic Burmese records as to the prevalence of the Mahāyāna or any other form of Buddhism before or after the Theravāda reformation of the eleventh century is apparently a serious difficulty for the historian to overcome. But, "this is merely a sectarian endeavour", as M. Duroiselle rightly points out, "to make the nation forget that there had once existed at Pagan a Buddhist sect outside the pale of Sinhalese Buddhism"[1].

The Problems Stated

The problems before us can now be stated as follows:

1. What is the earliest form of Sanskrit Buddhism in Burma, and where did it thrive?
2. What is the significance of Sanskrit inscriptions found in Pagan and other places in Upper Burma, and of Sanskrit texts referred to in inscriptions? Is there any evidence of the existence of Mahāyānist and Tantric texts in Burma? If so, what is their significance?
3. What is the conclusion to be derived from archaeological finds that can definitely be labelled as belonging to the Mahāyāna and other later schools of Sanskrit Buddhism?
4. Who were the Aris? Who were the Samaṇakuṭṭakas? And in what way are they related with the Mahāyāna or Mahāyānist Tantric cults of Buddhism?
5. What is the testimony of Indian documents regarding the introduction of the Mahāyāna and other allied cults into Burma, and what evident conclusions can be derived from them?

---

1. Duroiselle, *op. cit.*

6. When and whence did these cults of Sanskrit Buddhism penetrate Burma? And, finally,
7. What was the relative position of the orthodox and heterodox schools of Buddhsim in Burma? Did the latter influence the former in any way?

These problems will now be discussed one by one in the following chapters.

1
Sarvāstivāda in Ancient Prome

Sanskrit Inscriptions from Old Prome: Their Significance

In the course of excavations carried out at Karl-wet-khaung-kọn in Old Prome in 1927-28, M. Duroiselle came upon a very interesting bilingual inscription incised on the three sides of the pedestal of a Buddha image seated in the *dhyāna-mudrā and vajraparyaṅka* attitude. The record is composed in beautiful Sanskrit verse, but is interspersed with what Dr. Blagden has recognized as Pyu renderings of the Sanskrit text; the script is later Gupta-Brāhmī of Eastern India of about the seventh century; and the image itself can stylistically be ascribed to the later Gupta tradition of art, belonging to exactly the same period as is suggested by the palaeography of the inscription[1]. The image seems to have been set up by King Jayacandravarman at the instance of his religious teacher *(guru)* with the express purpose of establishing and enhancing peace, amity and good-will between the king himself and his younger brother *(tasyānuja)* Harivikrama. Jayacandra, further it is stated in the record, built two cities *(puradvayam)* side by side (evidently, one for each) and even in one day *(ekaika divase).*

The record is valuable in more then one respect. It supplies us with a definite starting-point in the political history of ancient Prome, and yields important information regarding the history of

1. This important record, the first of its kind in Burma, still remains unpublished, though a notice of the find appeared in the *An, R.A.S.I.* as early as 1927-28, pp. 128, 145. The courtesy of Mr. K. N. Dikshit, Deputy Director-General of Archaeology in India, and of Dr. C. O. Blagden has enabled me to study the record, a summary of the results of which I am incorporating here. I take this opportunity of acknowledging with thanks the kindness of these two scholars.

Buddhism in Lower Burma about the seventh century A.D., besides contributing substantially to the elucidation of the origin of the Pyu script. So far as the present study is concerned, the Prome inscription allows us to arrive at some tentative conclusions: (1) there seems to have existed a certain rivalry between the two brothers, Jayacandravarman and Harivikrama, and the former was advised to put an end to it, by providing two cities, one for each, so as to promote peace and goodwill between the two brothers; (2) Jayacandravarman and Harivikrama both belonged to one and the same dynasty, not to two different families, as has been generally supposed, by reason of their having two different name-endings; (3) the royal house to which these two brothers belonged adhered to Buddhism; and 4) what is most important, the Buddhism professed by Jayacandravarman belonged to one of the Northern Schools whose canons are supposed to have been written in Sanskrit.

The second inportant Sanskrit inscription recovered from the Tuins of Hmawza is found on the pedestal of a headless Buddha image[1], and consists of the well-known Buddhist formula *ye dharmā hetuprabhavā* . . . etc., which used to be widely inscribed on terracotta tablets all over Burma, in Sanskrit as well as in Pāli. The script of the record is the same as that of the Prome inscription noted above, *viz.*, it is North-Eastern Indian Brāhmi of about the seventh century. The style of the image agrees with that of the Buddha image from Kan-wet-khaung-kon; it represents the late Gupta tradition of Eastern India.

These two are not the only images belonging to this art tradition which were recovered from the ruins of Prome. In fact, these ruins have recently yielded a large number of stone sculptures and terracotta reliefs, mostly representing Buddhist subjects, and belonging to an art-tradition familiar in Magadha during the 6th-8th centuries. Nor are these epigraphic records the only ones found at Hmawza. This locality has produced a large number of terracotta votive tablets inscribed with the Buddhist formula in late Gupta Brāhmi characters of about the 7th and 8th centuries. Some of them have evidently been brought to Burma by pious folowers of the faith from such Indian centres of Buddhism as Sārnāth and

---

1. *An, R.A.S.I.*, 1928-29, p. 108, pl. IIb.

Bodh-gayā; others were certainly moulded and inscribed by local Craftsmen for local requirements, as they bear on them Pyu words and legends as well.

The original home of these records and images is then North Eastern India, *i.e.*, the Magadhan region. It will be remembered that this region, in the seventh century was a stronghold of the Sarvāstivāda-nikāya, as is testified by I-tsing[1], and probably also by Hiuen Thsang when he speaks of the "Mahāyānist of the Sthavira School" in Magadha[2]. From this fact we infer that the

---

1. Takakusu, *I-tsing's Records.*, pp. xxii, 8.
2. Watters, *Yuan Chwang*, II, p. 136, and comments on pp. 138, 198, 234-35 and 248.

It is uncertain what Hiuen Thsang exactly means by the expression "Mahāyānist of the Sthavira school", which involves an apparent contradiction. Hiuen Thsang, moreover, is not very definite in his description of the various schools of Buddhism prevalent in his time. The term 'Mahāyānist' he uses in a very loose sense; even the Buddhist brethren of Ceylon be calls "Mahāyānist Sthavira". The Sthaviravādins or Theravādins were a Hīnayānist sect, and although the Mahāyānists followed the Vinaya of the Theravādins, the closest relation of the Theravādins lay, of all the Northern Buddhist sects, with the Sarvāstivādins who, like the Theravādins, were recognized as a Hinayānist sect and who also followed the Vinaya of the Theravādins. I am therefore disposed to assume that by his phrase, "Mahāyānists of the Sthavira school", Hiuen Thsang probably referred to those Buddhists of the Northern School who were recognized as Hinayānists, and had thus the closest relation with the Sthaviravādins, but whose canonical language, in common with the Mahāyānists, was Sanskrit, *viz.*, the Sarvāstivādins.

My main reason for equating the "Mahāyānists of the Sthavira School" with the Sarvāstivādins is this: Hiuen Thsang describes the Buddhist brethren of the Mahābodhi Vihāra as "Mahāyānists of the Sthavira School", and Watters in his note observes that "at his time many of the brethren in the Magadban monasteries were evidently Mahāyānists in that sense" (II, p. 138). It is also significant that I-tsing who comes only about 25 years later states that "in Magadha .... the Sarvāstivāda-nilkāya flourishes the most" (Takakusu, *op. cit.*, p. 8). This is upheld also by the parallel statements of the two pilgrims with regard to Kalinga. According to the older pilgrim, the brethren of the monasteries of Ka-lang-ka (Kaliṅga) were "students of the Mahāyānist Sthavira school" (Watters, *op. cit.*, p. I98). According to I-tsing, the Mūlasarvāstivāda-nikāya was also adopted in Kaliṅga. And I-tsing himself being a Sarvāstivādin could not have been mistaken on this point.

Buddhism represented by the inscribed images of Prome was that of the Mūlasarvāstivādins.

One may at once ask: why not of the Mahāyānists? There is nothing definitely to refute such a question, but considering the very paucity of finds, definitely Mahāyānist, recovered from Old Prome, and from the very powerful influence that Hīnayāna exercised there from about two centuries earlier, it seems unlikely that the Mahāyāna had any such popularity at so early a date as to warrant our assuming the existence of a Mahāyānist family of kings and the find of a number of Sanskrit inscriptions including the long record from Kan-wet-khaung-kon.

The main argument for ascribing this Sanskrit Buddhism of Old Prome to the Sarvāstivāda is the language. The second point is the script and the art-tradition of the images which bear these records, and the third, the locality from where this Buddhism seems to have travelled to Burma. The Pāli epigraphs found at the old capital of Prome are all written in what is called the Kānāḍā Telegu or Kadamba script, and are unmistakably records of Theravāda Buddhism, while the Sanskrit epigraphs, are invariably in a North-East Indian script, *viz.*, in late Gupta-Brāhmī or early Nāgarī of Eastern India. We know that the Theravāda and the Sarvāstivāda differ but little in principle and almost nothing in practice; both of them belong to the broader Hīnayāna and follow the same *Vinaya*. It is therefore only likely that the Buddhism represented by these Sanskrit documents of ancient Prome can be the Sarvāstivāda. We only suggest it as a probable explanation of the use of Sanskrit in frankly Buddhist, presumably Hīnayānist, records. This, I think cannot be explained by the fact of the presence of Brahmins and Brahmanical Hinduism at the capital, of the old kingdom of Prome[1], or even by stray finds of Mahāyāna images there, none of which can be dated, on account of the style, before the eighth or ninth century.

Significance of I-Tsing's Evidence

This assumption of the existence of Sarvāstivāda in ancient Prome during the seventh and eighth centuries seem to find striking

1. See, my *Brahmanical Gods* . . . ., Calcutta University, 1932.

support from what I-tsing states about the relative position of the different schools of Buddhism in his time in the islands of the Southern Sea.

This celebrated Chinese traveller sojourned in India and the Eastern Archipelago in the last quarter of the seventh century (671-95), the same period to which the Buddhist Sanskrit inscription and images may paleographically and stylistically be assigned. It is unfortunate that the pilgrim did not visit any of the regions situated along the sea-coast of Burma or at some distance in the interior. But he certainly took pains to learn about the state of the religion in all these countries lying to the east and south of the Bay[1]. That he succeeded to a great extent is proved by the following passage in his *Nan hai chi kuei Nai fa ch'en* (ch. I, f. 3, verso).

> At the (eastern) extremity (of the eastern frontier countries, i.e., East India) there is the so called Great Black Mountain which is, I think, on the Southern boundary of Tufan (Tibet, according to Takakusu]. This mountain is said to be on the South-west of Shu-chuan (Ssu Ch'uan) from which one can reach this mountain after a journey of a month or so, Southward from this, and, close to the sea-coast there is a country called Shih-li-ch'a-ta-lo (Śrīkṣetra); on the south-east of these is Langchia-shu (Laṅkāsu); on the east is She-ho-po-ti (Dvāravatī); at the extreme cast Lin-i. The inhabitants of all these countries greatly reverence the Three Gems [evidently, the Buddha, Dharma and Saṁgha]. There are many who hold firmly to the precepts and perform the begging *dhūta* which constitutes a custom in these countries[2].

Of the countries mentioned in the above passage. Lin-i has been identified with Campa, She-ho-po-ti with Dvāravatī (now Ayuthia in Siam), Shih-li-ch'a-ta-lo with Śrīkṣetra or Old Prome" (the capital now being represented by the ruins of Hmawza), and Lang-chia-shu with the kingdom of Chia-mo-lang-chia or Kāmalaṅka of Hiuen Thsang[3]. The identifications of Lin-i, She-ho-po-ti (also mentioned by Hiuen Thsang as To-lo-po-ti) and Shih-li-ch'a-ta-lo has also been mentioned by Hiuen Thsang as situated to the north-east

1. Takakusu, *op. cit.*, p. 8-11.
2. Takausu, *op. cit.*, pp. 9-10; Pelliot, *B.E.F.E.O.*, 1904, pp. 405-06; Chavannes, *Religieux Eminents*, p. 58, n.
3. For these identifications see, Takakusu, *op. cit.*, pp. li-lii; Phayre, *History of Burma*, p. 32; Beal, *Buddhist Records of the Western World*, II, p. 200, n. 34: Chavannes, *op. cit.*, and above all, Pelliot, "Deux Itineraires", in *B.E.F.E.O.*, 1904.

of Samataṭa, by the side of a great sea in a valley of mountains. This orientation of Śrīkṣetra is evidently wrong; for it lies far to the south-east, not to the north-east of Samataṭa[1].

Identification of Lang-Chia-Shu

The identification of the one remaining name, Lang-chia-shu or Laikāsu, has long puzzled scholars. It is generally assumed that I-tsing's Lang-chia-shu is the same as Hiuen Thsang's Chia-mo-lang-chia or Kāmalaṅka, because Lang-chia-shu is placed by I-tsing exactly in the same relation to Śrīkṣetra and Dvāravatī as Chia-mo-lang-chia is placed by Hiuen Thsang in relation to the same kingdoms[2]. We may therefore assume that they are one and the same country; nor can there be any objection to their being identified, as Messers Phayre and Beal do[3], with Pegu and the deltaic region of the Irrawady. But as Lang-chia-shu has been identified with a considerable number of similar names found in Chinese and other sources, there exists the possibility of the kingdom being identified with other regions of Further India. It has been pointed out that Lang-chia or Lang-chia-shu is mentioned several times by I-tsing as a port visited by Chinese pilgrims (whose lives he records) on their way to India[4].

It seems clear that I-tsing's Lang-chia (-shu) "was on the west coast of the Peninsula, on the route somewhere between Annam and Java; and if so, how can it be both south-east of Śrīkṣetra and west of Dvāravatī which is placed in the basin of the Menam? I-tsing, when he sent his *Lives of the Pilgrims* back to China, had lived about eight years in the seas of the South, mostly at Palembang. Could he have made any mistake about the position of Langchia-shu . . .? Or, did he know, without troubling to distinguish them, two kingdoms of the name of Lang-chia (-shu), the one somewhere in Tennasserim, the other on the east side of the Peninsula

1. Luce, *J.B.R.S.*, XIV. II. p. 161.
2. "Thence north-east (i.e., from Samatata) beside the great sea in a valley of hills is the kingdom of Shih-li-ch'a-ta-lo; thence to the south-east, in a corner of the great sea is the kingdom of Chia-mo-lang-chia; thence in the east, is the kingdom of To-lo-po-ti". This is from Hiuen Thsang's Records; compare it with that of I-tsing quoted above.
3. *op. cit.*
4. One such passage may be found in Chavannes, *op. cit.*, p. 100.

south of the isthmus of Kra? Or, is I-tsing here merely echoing Hiuen Thsang, but substituting for Kāmalaṅka (a name unknown to him), one that was familar, Lang-chia-shu, without much regard for geographical accuracy"1 ?

Meanwhile, Lang-chia-shu has been taken to be identical with the kingdom of Lang-ya or Lang-ya-hsun which is referred to in the *Liang shu* (ch. 54, f. 3, verso), and also with that of Lang-yahsü mentioned in connection with Ch'ang Chun's embassy to Ch'ih-t'u kingdom in 607-08 A.D. (*Pei Shih*, ch. 13, f. 3, recto; *Sui shu,* chap. 82, f. 1, verso)[2]. Without going into the details of these texts which have been ably discussed by Drs. Chavannes, Schlegel, Pelliot and Mr. Luce[3], it may be said that the position of these kingdoms, as described in the Chinese texts, seems to be quite in accordance with that of I-tsing's Lang-chia-shu, i.e., they are situated somewhere on the east coast of the Malay Peninsula to the south of the isthmus of Kra.

Futhermore, Lang-chia-shu has also been identified with Ling yu-Ssŭ-chia mentioned by Chau-ju-kua (1225)[4], as one of the fifteen dependencies of San-fo-ch'i (Śrīvijaya = Sumatra = Palembang), which again, M. Coedès thinks[5], is the same as (a) Ilaṅgāsogam of Tanjore Tamil inscription of Rājendracola (1012-1042), and (b) the Lĕnkasuka, a dependency of Majapahit, mentioned in the Kawi poem *Nāgarakrĕtāgama* (14th century). M. Pelliot conjectures that Lang-chia-shu = Lang-ya-hsiu =Lang-ya-hsŭ=Lingyu-ssŭ (-chia) = Lĕnkasuka was one and the same kingdom[6] which he identified with Tennasserim. M. Ferrand agrees with him but further identifies it with Ilaṅgāsogam, the Locac of Marco Polo[7] (end of the 13th century), and finally with Lang-sakā of of an Arabic manuscript of the 16th century, situated on

---

1. Luce, J.B.R.S., *op. cit.*, pp. 162-63.
2. Luce, *ibid*, pp. 164-65.
3. Pelliot, *op. cit.*, *B.E.F.E.O.*, 1903 and 1904; Chavannes, *op. cit.*; Schlegel T'*oung Pao,* IX, P. 193; Luce, *op. cit.*
4. Chau-ju-kua, ed. by Hirth and Rockhill. This kingdom is also referred to as Ling-ya-ssŭ.
5. Coedès, *B.E.F.E.O.*, 1918, no. 6.
6. *B.E.F.E.O.*, 1904, pp. 405-407.
7. Yule and Cordier's edn. II, p. 276.

the east of the Malay Peninsula[1]. He therefore fixes the position of the kingdom on the isthmus of Ligor. But Coedès, while finding in Lang-chia-shu of I-tsing Lang-ya-hsiu of the *Liang-shu* and the Lang-ya-hsu of the *Sui shu* one and the same place, sees in the Ilaṅgāsogam of Rājendracola's inscription, the Ling-ya-ssŭ-chia of Chau-ju-kua and the Lĕnkasuka of the *Nāgarakrĕtāgama* quite a different place[2]. He identifies the former with Tennasserim just as M. Pelliot does, and the latter with Gunong Jĕrai or Kedah Peak, in the south of the Kedah State.

We have surveyed the various identifications proposed of I-tsing's Lang-chia-shu. None of them is free from objections. M. Pelliot was obviously influenced by the fact that I-tsing located the kingdom south-east of Śrīkṣetra and west of Dvāravatī, a circumstance which cannot be ignored. M. Ferrand's arguments for placing it on the isthmus of Ligor are hardly convincing; his identification does neither suit the statement that it was situated southeast of Śrīkṣetra and west of Dvāravatī, nor the fact which I-tsing elsewhere seems to indicate, according to some, that it was on the opposite coast of the Peninsula some-where on the route between Annam and Java. The first identification of M. Coedès where he agrees with M. Pelliot conforms to the statement of I-tsing about its location, but the distinction he makes between the two sets of names is open to objections which have rightly been pointed out by Mr. Luce[3].

For the present, I am rather disposed to agree with M. Pelliot, and identify I-tsing's Lang-chia (-shu) with at least that portion of the present Tennasserim division which extends from Tavoy to Tennasserim proper, i.e., the region watered by the Tennasserim river, which is really to the south-east of Śrikṣetra and west of Dvāravatī. Personally, I feel inclined to assume that Lang-chia-shu was practically identical with the entire Tennasserim division of to-day extending from Thaton to Tennasserim. The position, then, of the various kingdoms bordering the Southern Sea may be stated briefly as follows: first, Shih-li-ch'a-ta-lo or Śrikṣetra;

1. *J.A.*, Juit-Aout, 1918, pp. 134-45, 153-54.
2. "A translation of the Kedah Annals", in the *J. Ind. Arch.*, III, p. 11-13.
3. *J.B.R.S.*, XIV, ii, pp. 168-69.

second, Lang-chia-shu or Chia-mo-lang-chia or Kāmalaṅka to the south-west of Śrīkṣetra and west of Dvāravatī; third, She-ho-po-ti or To-lo-po-ti (= Dvāravatī); fourth, P'an-p'an to the south of Dvāravatī and south-west of Lin-i (Campa), 'in a corner of the sea'; fifth, Chen-la or Old Fou-nan (Kamboja), to the east southeast of P'an-p'an; and lastly, Lin-i to the extreme east extending as far as the coast.

As for other references by I-tsing[1] to Lang-chia-shu, I think, they can be reconciled in the following way: the boats that carried the Chinese Buddhist pilgrims kept generally to the coast-line till they passed Fou-nan (or Chen-la, as it was then called), whence they did no longer follow the coast-line, but favoured by the current, crossed the Gulf of Siam, almost diagonally, till they came to anchor somewhere at the head of the Gulf on the east coast of the Peninsula, whence they crossed over to Ho-ling (Java), and thence *via* Nikobar to Tāmralipti. For the rest, we can safely assume that the kingdom of Lang-chia-shu extended from coast to coast of the Peninsula.

We are now in a position to use more or less definitely I-tsing's data as to the state of Buddhism in the countries in question. Of the various countries in Further India that practised Buddhism in his time, one, viz., Śrīkṣetra, is definitely included in Burma; and the other, Lang-chia-shu, too, we have tentatively indentified with a region included in the same territory. According to I-tsing, 'the inhabitants of both these countries, greatly reverenced the Three Gems, and held firmly to the precepts, and performed the begging *dhūta* that constituted a custom in these countries'. In one of the countries, namely, Lang-chia-shu, Buddhist preists from China used to be received in those days with honour, as will be evident from the following passage which is quoted on the authority of Chavannes:

> I-lang, Chih-ngan and I-hsian, three Chinese pilgrims having reached We-Lei (a small sea-port west of Pakhoi in Canton) sailed on a merchant ship. . . . They passed Fu-nan, and anchored in the country of Lang-chia-shu; and were treated by the king of that country with ceremony that is usually accorded to very honoured and distinguished guests[2].

1. Chavannes, *op. cit.*, pp. 57, 78, 100.
2. Ibid., p. 57.

Taolin, another Chinese pilgrim, whom we have had occasion to mention, also visited the same kingdom; he too was welcomed by the king of the country with the greatest courtesy, and was treated with utmost care and respect[1].

It now remains to be considered to which school this Buddhism of Śrīkṣetra and Lang-chia-shu really belonged. On this point I-tsing himself, I think, gives us a very illuminating, and almost a definite lead. He speaks of the four nikāyas or schools of Buddhism in his time: the Mahāsaṁghika-nikāya, the Sthavira-nikāya, the Sammiti-nikāya and the Mūlasarvāstivāda-nikāya; "but the number of votaries in each school is unequal in different places". As to the distribution of the different schools, he states:

> In Magadha the doctrines of the four nikāyas are generally in practice, *yet the Saruāstivāda-nikāya flourishes the most.* In Lāṭa and Sindhu, the names of countries in Western India, the Sammiti-nikāya has the greater number of followers, and there are some few members of the other three schools. In *the Northern Region all belong to the Sarvāsti-vāda-nikāya,* though we sometimes meet with the followers of the Mahāsaṁghikanikāya. Towards the South all follow the Sthavira-nikāya though there exist a few adherents of the other four nikāyas. In the Eastern Frontier Countries, the four nikāyas are found side by side. ... In the Siṁhala island all belong to the Ārya Sthavira-nikāya, and the Ārya Mahāsaṁghika-nikāya is rejected. *In the islands of the Southern Sea, consisting of more than ten countries, the Mūlasarvāstivāda-nikāya has been almost universally adopted,* though occasionally some have devoted themselves to the Sammiti-nikāya, and recently a few followers of the other two schools have also been found. Counting from the west, there is first of all P'o-lu-shih chou (i.e., Baros, northwest of Sumatra), and then Molo-yu chou (probably Jambi, north of Palembang) which is now the kingdom of Shih-li-fo-shih (Śrīvijaya), Mo-ho-hsin chou[2], Ho-ling chou (in Java), Ta-ta chou (probably Tan-tan), P'én-p'ĕn chou (perhaps modern Pembuan on the southern coast of Borneo), P'o-li chou (Bali).

1. Chavannes, *op.cit.,* p. 100.
2. Pelliot finds in it the Mo-ho-hsin kingdom of the *T'ai p'ing huan yū chi.* "In one of the inscriptions", says M. Pelliot, "of the Javanese King Erlaṅga ... there is mention of a war led by this prince against the king of Mabasin", *B.E.F.E.O.*, 1904, pp. 325, 362, Mr. Takakusu sought to identify it with Bandjermasin in South Borneo (*Records*, p. xivll). Mr. Winstedt following Mr. Rouffaer, identified it with Singapur of the 15th and Johor of the 16th century (*St. Br. As. Soc. Jour.*, no. 86, Nov. 1922, p. 258. For M. Ferrand's views, see, *J.A.*, 1919, pp. 298-99.

K'u-lun chou[1], Fo-shih-pu-lo chou[2]), A-shan chou (not identified), and Mo-chia-man chou[3]. There are some more islands which cannot all be Imentioned here. Buddhism is embraced in all these countries, and mostly the Hīnayāna is adopted, except in Mo-lo-yu, where there are a few who belong to the Mahāyāna[4].

The Buddhism of Shih-Li-Ch'a-Ta-Lo and Lang-Chia-Shu

We have seen above that I-tsing speaks of the definite existence of Buddhism in Shih-li-ch'a-ta-lo, Lang-chia-shu, She-ho-po-ti and Lin-i, but he does not say to which particular nikāya this Buddhism belonged, though he asserts that they all subscribed to the Hīnayāna. Now, we know that all the three nikāyas, the Ārya Sthavira-nikāya, the Ārya Sammiti-nikāya and the Ārya Mūlasarvāstivāda-nikāya, are comprised within the Hīnayāna. To which of these nikāyas, then, of the Hīnayāna, must we ascribe the Buddhism of Shih-li-ch'a-ta-lo and Lang-chia-shu? We have only One possible answer to this question, I think; it belonged to the Mūlasarvāstivāda-nikāya. Of the three nikāyas, the Sthaviravāda is ruled out as it was practised only in Ceylon and to some extent in the south of India. The Sammiti-nikāya is also similarly ruled out, because it had its largest number of followers in the Lāṭa and Sindhu countries, though in the islands of the Southern Sea, (e.g., in Campa) *occasionally* there were a handful of followers of this school. In all other realms of the Buddhist world, excepting the Divine Land or Red province (i.e., China), it was the Mūlasarvāstivāda-nikāya that was *universally* practised. It is thus only in the logic of facts, considering the wide prevalence of the Sarvāstivāda in

---

1. According to M. Ferrand, it stands for Gulun or Gurun, mentioned as a toponym in the *Nāgarakrĕtāgama;* perhaps it is the island of Goron or Goram, to the south-east of the island of Ceram. (Ferrand, *J.A.*, 1919, pp. 301-02).
2. Mr. Takakusu and M. Ferrand sought to identify it with Bhojanagara in north-east of Java, but the latter points out that, if so, I-tsing is not observing his arrangement, from west to east.
3. The *Nāgarakrĕtāgama* mentions a Markkaman which Dr. Krom places to the south of Pasuruan. Ferrand, *J.A.*, 1919, p. 302.
4. Takakusu, *op. cit.*, pp. 8-10; also see Luce, *J.B.R.S.* XIV, ii, 1924. pp. 202-205; the rendering in both are almost the same, but Mr. Luce gives better identification of place-names.

I-tsing's time[1], that the Buddhism of Shih-li-ch'a-talo and Langchia-shu cannot be other than the Sarvāstivāda itself. This almost obvious conclusion is vested with a significance when we bear in mind I-tsing's important statement that 'in the islands of the Southern Sea (which included Borneo, Sumatra, Java and the Malaya Peninsula) the Mūlasarvāstivāda-nikāya has been universally accepted.'

With regard to Shih-li-ch'a-ta-lo, there is moreover the evidence of the inscriptions. I-tsing tells us that the Buddhism of these countries was the Hīnayāna. We have two sets of Buddhist epigraphic records from the ancient city of Prome (= I-tsing's Shih-li-ch'a-ta-lo);one is in Pāli written in Kadamba or Kānāḍā-Telegu characters and belonging to a period not later than the sixth century; the other in Sanskrit written in later Gupta-Brāhmī characters of about the seventh century. We know that the Pāli records are ascribed to the Theravāda; and to what other school of the Hīnayāna the Sanskrit records may possibly belong than to the Sarvāstivāda?

This Sarvāstivāda of Lower Burma, it has been suggested above, came from the Magadhan region of North-Eastern India which in the seventh century was itself one of the strongest centres of the Mūlasarvāstivāda-nikāya.

---

1. "In I-tsing's time, the Sarvāstivāda school flourished most in North India and in Magadha and Central India (Madhyadeśa), and had also some followers in the East and West; but was entirely absent in Ceylon, and had very few adherents in South India. No other school, so far as we can ascertain, ever flourished so widely as the Sarvāstivāda, either before or after the seventh century, though its adherents in India alone, in Hiuen Thsang's time, were not so numerous as those of other schools". Takakusu, *J.R.A.S.*, 1891, P. 420; also, *Records*, p. xxii.

2
Sanskrit Inscriptions: Sanskrit Buddhist Texts

I

Sanskrit Inscriptions from Upper Burma: Their Significance

Every year archaeological excavation in Pagan and at other ancient sites of Upper Burma brings to light a number of stone sculptures and terracotta votive tablets with or without figures of the Buddha and attendants, so that there is now an enormous number of them in the collection of the Archaeological Survey of Burma. These objects invariably are inscribed with a short legend which in nearly every case is the well-known Buddhist formula, *ye dharmā hetuprabhavā* ..., written in mediaeval Nāgarī, and sometimes in proto-Bengali characters of the 9th-13th centuries. Evidently the great majority of these inscribed tablets were brought from the East Indian countries of Bihar and Bengal to Pagan and other important centres of Burma, but some of them were moulded locally, for, they bear the names of royal and other personages of Pagan. The language is mostly Sanskrit; sometimes the legends are in Pāli or mixed Sanskrit and Pāli, but here we are mainly concerned with those in Sanskrit. Among those moulded locally and bearing local names, we have a considerable number, containing the name of the great Pagan king Mahārāja Śri Aniruddhadeva (i.e., king Anawrahta). But those tablets are not at the same time inscribed with the Buddhist creed. To quote a few examples:

1. *Saccakadānapati-Mahārāja-Śrī-Aniruddhadevena kato ayam.*
2. *Saddharmo'yam saccadānapati-Mahārāja-Śrī-Aniruddhadevena...*
3. *Eso bhagavā Mahārāja-Śrī-Aniruddhadevena kato vimuttattham sahattheneva ti.*

4. *Mayāniruddhadevena kṛtam Sugata-s[aṁ]ccakam, tena Maitreya Sambodho labheyan nivṛtto [?] padam*[1].

Similar legends, but associated with the names of other persons are inscribed on votive tablets which have also been found among the ruins of Pagan and other centres in Upper Burma. The following is an example:

Mayā [Śri] Ru [dra]-devena kṛta[m] [Suga] ta [sa] [ṁ]ccakam, tena Maitreyam-aṃvo[bho] [dhan] labheyan niruṛtan padam[2].

It will at once be seen that these legends are written in mixed Sanskrit and Pāli. But quite a large number of them are in pure Sanskrit, though they contain nothing besides the Buddhist formula. But whatever may be the language, the script is always the same; it is mediaeval Nāgarī and proto-Bengali of the period which we have suggested.

This can lead to one conclusion alone, and it is this: some sort of Buddhism of the northern variety, with Sanskrit as vehicle of expression must have been in existence *already before,* and *even after*, the introduction of Therevāda Buddhism from Thaton by Anawrahta in 1057 froln which time Sanskrit was gradually superseded by Pāli[3]. It has long been recognized that Sanskrit was known in Pagan as the language of Brahmanical Hinduism and of Brahmin court-astrologers and priests. In fact, Brahmanical and Sanskritic elements are abundantly clear in the Mon inscriptions of Burma. But the use of the same language in what are definitely Buddhist objects of worship cannot but lead to the conclusion just arrived at[4], and the use of the Eastern Nāgarī and proto-Bengali character lends support to the assumption. These scripts were the only varieties used during the 9th-13th centuries in the modern provinces

1. *An. R.A.S.B.*, 1915, p. 16; *An. R.A.S.I.*, 1926-27, pp. 161-62. Votive tablets with one or other of these and similar legends bearing the name of Aniruddhadeva have been found in temples and stūpas built by Anawrahta himself.
2. *An. R.A.S.B.*, 1916, p. 39.
3. This is probably reflected in the half-Pāli half-Sanskrit language of the inscriptions.
4. "... It can easily be proved that Sanskrit works, Mahāyānist and probably also Sanskrit Hinayānist and Brahmanical works, were in use at Pagan before Anorata".- Duroiselle, *Ep. Birm.*, I.i, p. 7. No proof however is given, though the fact is now recognized by all.

of Bengal and Bihar whence most of the tablets must have been brought to Burma[1]; even those that were moulded locally slavishly imitated Indian models from Sārnāth, Bodh-gayā, Nālandā and other centres as far east as Tipperah in Eastern Bengal. These two countries, particularly the ancient Magadha country, were, in I-tsing's time, as we have seen, strongholds of the Sarvāstivāda, but already from the eighth and ninth centuries onwards, came to be dominated almost wholly by the Mahāyāna. Such parallel transition in the history of Buddhism we have also noticed in Further India and Indonesia[2]. It is therefore probable that the Sanskrit Buddhism of Pagan, as evidenced in the writings of the votive tablets, belonged to the Mahāyāna. This conclusion is confirmed by the writings of Tibetan scholars, notably Tāranātha, to which we shall have occasion to revert.

Sanskrit Buddhism seems to have had a foothold in Pagan for at least two centuries - some of these tablets can paleographically be dated about the ninth century - when the Theravāda came to measure strength with it. We shall see that this conclusion, drawn from a study of the inscriptions, is corroborated not only by Burmese historical tradition as recorded in the chronicles, but also by literary and archaeological evidence.

II

Sanskrit Texts of Mahāyāna and Tantrayāna

It has been long recognized that Sanskrit texts, mostly Brahmanical,

---

1. Some of these tablets are often as late as the 12th and 13th century, but the later ones, though written in the same Nāgarī or proto-Bengali characters, are mostly in Pālī, showing no doubt the increasing influence of the Theravāda. Buddhism following the great religious upheaval after the Conquest of Thaton. With regard to the importance of the tablets bearing legends in Sanskrit, M. Duroiselle says: "They point to an active intercourse between Burma and Northern India. . . . They coroborate the tradition, duly recorded in chronicles, that Singalese Buddhism (meaning probably Theravāda Buddhism] did not exist in Pagan before Anawrahta, or at least, that it was not yet followed by the majority of the people who professed Mahāyānism and, which is also very probable, a form of Hinayānism the scriptures of which are written in Sanskrit". *An. R.A.S.B.*, 1913, p. 17.
2. See, *supra,* chap. I.

were known in Burma. These texts related to such secular subjects as astrology, astronomy, medicine, rhetoric, poetics, law, political and military science, etc. They also included works on Brahmanical Tantras and Kāmaśāstras. That a store of Sanskrit learning existed from very early times jealously guarded by Brahmanical priests, court-astronomers, and counsellors and minsters of the realm residing at the court of the Burmese kings was first pointed out by that pioneer scholar of Burmese antiquities, Mr. Forchammer[1]. He wrote as early as 1880, "There exists a real Sanskrit literature in Burma written on paper like India with Nāgarī and Bengali characters. These records are in the hands of the descendants of Hindu colonists who at different periods, some even before the spread of Buddhism in Burma, settled in this country. . . Burma derserves to be drawn within the circle of those countries where researches of Sanskrit records ought to be made"[2].

Brahmanism and Sanskrit Learning

Already in the eighties of the last century, Mr. Forchammer collected a number of inscriptions from Pagan, Pinya and Ava[3], including one, dated B.E. 804 = 1442 A.D., which commemorates the bestowal of a monastery with a garden, paddy lands, slaves, and what is most important, a large collection of texts (numbering 295) upon the Buddhist Order by the governor of Taungdwin and his wife[4]. The catalogue of books which is given in the inscription is extremely interesting as it shows in which subjects the monks were most interested and what was the general trend of their studies. As the list has been reproduced more than once[5], we need not quote

1. Jardine, *Notes on Buddhist Law*, IV., Introduction by Forchammer, p. 17: also, Forchammer, *Report of Literary Work*, 1879-80, pp. 6 ff.
2. Forchammer, *ibid*, p. 13.
3. *Inscriptions of Pagan, Pinya and Ava*. Deciphered from the ink impressions found among Forchammer's papers, Rangoon, 1902.
4. Such gifts of books are recorded in an inscription in Burma, but the most interesting thing of this inscription is that here we have one solitary example where a complete list of books is catalogued.
5. E.g., Bode, *Pāli Literature of Burma*, pp. 101 ff. Pelliot, "Deux Itineraires", in *B.E.F.E.O.*, 1904. V, p. 183: Ray, *History of Buddhism in Burma*, chap. III.

it again. "We notice here", Dr. Mabel Bode remarks, "a number of titles of Sanskrit works, sometimes greatly disguised in the Burmese transcription, but still recognisable. These will aid us to form some notion of the point reached by the Sanskrit scholars in Burma in the fifteenth century. We are not obliged to believe that each monastery contained students of Sanskrit, but we have at least some grounds for supposing that certain famous works on grammar, prosody, medicine and so forth were treasured in Upper Burma"[1].

The inscription proves that even Buddhist monks were interested in essentially Brahmanical texts on secular subjects; we may assume that they did study these texts along with their own sacred writings, as is proved not only by a considerable number of Burmese translations of several Sanskrit works but also by the honorific epithet *Vedasatthakovida* ("expert in *Vedasatthas*") which was sometimes conferred on certain monks. The *Sāsanavaṁsa*[2] repeatedly refers to monks who were experts in *Vedasatthas* which, however, had nothing to do with Vedic texts, or even with Brahmanical religious literature. The term "Vedasattha" was used by Burmese monks to designate texts on astronomy, astrology, law, polity, medicine, lexicography, grammar, rhetoric etc.[3]. We do not know, what contemporary opinion thought of these *Vedasatthakovidas;* but subsequently orthodox opinion, as represented by Paññasāmī, the author of the *Sāsanavaṁsa*, did not hold them in respect; at least a certain section of the monastic order did not favour this Brahmanical learning. In fact, if the *Sāsanavaṁsa* is to be believed, the Order frankly disapproved of them. According to Paññasāmi, these *Vedasatthakovidas* were deficient in the knowledge and practice of the religion *(pariyattipaṭipattiste mandā)*, and the ancient chroniclers did not consider them worthy of being reckoned in the *theraparamparā (theraparamparāya na gaṇenti porāṇā)*[4].

There is a point which is still more important in this catalogue and which has hitherto escaped the notice of scholars. This list contains at least four works that can be traced to Mahāyānist Sanskrit

1. Bode, *op. cit.*
2. pp. 95, 105-109.
3. Jardine, *op. cit.*, Intro. by Forchammer, p. 17; Forchammer, *op. cit.*, p. 6. ff; Bode, *op. cit.*, pp. 50-51.
4. *Sāsana. . .*, p. 105.

texts, and at least three, if not five, works that are definitely Tantric. They are the following:

(a) 277. *Nyāya-bindu*
278. *Nyāya-bindu-ṭīkā*
279. *Hetu-bindu*
280. *Hetubindu-ṭīkā*

(b) 269. *Mṛtyuvañcana*
270. *Mahākālacakka*[1]
271. *Mahākālacakka-ṭīkā*[1]

Presumably there are two more texts in the list which are Tantric, though we cannot at present trace them to their Indian originals. They are:

194. *Rattamālā*[1] [duplicated in no. 294]
195. *Rattamālā-ṭīkā*[1]

Texts on Buddhist Logic

The *Nyāyabindu* and *Hetubindu* as well as the commentaries belonging to these two works are certainly treatises on Buddhist logic. The *Nyāyabindu* is the famous treatise on the subject by Ācārya Dharmakirti[2] (c. 635-650), a resident of South India in the kingdom of Cūḍāmaṇi (probably Coḷa or Coḍa country), and a disciple of Ācārya Dharmapāla. There are at least two commentaries on the *Nyāyabindu* called *Nyāyabindu-ṭīkā,* one by Vinītadeva (c. 675)[3] of Nālandā, and another by Ācārya Dharmottara of Kashmir (c. 850)[4]. The Sanskrit original of Vinītadeva's work is lost, but a Tibetan translation of it exists in the Tangyur, *Mdo*, She, folios I-43. The translation was due to the collaboration of the Indian scholar Jinamitra and his Tibetan colleague Vandeye-śses-sde. The original of Dharmottara's work was preserved in the Jaina temple of Śāntinātha, Cambay. It is difficult to decide which of these two texts is the one mentioned in the list. The *Hetubindu-ṭīkā*[5] is a

1. It is interesting that these four names are given in their Pāli form, whereas *Mṛtyuvañcana* is in correct Sanskrit form.
2. For Dharmakīrti and his works, see, for example, S.C. Vidyābhūṣaṇa, *Indian Logic; Mediaeval School,* pp. 103-118.
3. *Ibid.,* pp. 119-120.
4. *Ibid.,* p. 131.
5. *Ibid.,* p. 120.

detailed commentary on the *Hetubindu* of Dharmakīrti. The Sanskrit original of this work is lost, but there exists a Tibetan translation in the Tangyur, *Mdo*, She, folios 116-205; it was prepared as a result of the collaboration of Prajñāvarman and *D*pal-*br*tsegsrakṣita.

Buddhist logic is known to have developed among the brotherhood of those who owed their allegiance to the Mahāyāna and its allied creeds, and the above texts were works of Mahāyānist scholars. Their inclusion in a list in which Pāli works predominate, is, therefore, significant.

Tantric Texts

Three other books named above are definitely Tantric. We do not know of any Tantric Buddhist text called *Mṛtyuvañcana,* though evidently a text of the name must have existed. Its Tantric nature follows from the fact that the term "Mṛtyuvañcana" is employed to designate a well known theory peculiar to both Brahmanical and Buddhistic Tantric philosophy. "Mṛtyuvañcana" or *"kālasya vañcanam"* is a Tantric technical term and conveys invariably a Tantric meaning[1].

Mahākālacakka or Mahākālacakra and its ṭīkā must also have been Tantric texts. In the *Descriptive Catalogue of the Sanskrit Manuscripts in the Government Collection, A. S. Bengal,* we have two texts from Nepal catalogued as *Laghukālacakratantrarāja-ṭīkā* (no. 66) and *Langhukālacakra-ṭīkā* (no. 67), otherwise known as *Vimalaprabhā*[2]. The two *Laghus* naturally presuppose the existence of a *Mahākālacakra* and a *Mahākālacakra-ṭīkā* which are exactly the titles included in our list[3]. Kālacakra texts are definitely

1. For *"Rālasya vañcanam",* see Bagchi, *Kaulajñāna nirṇaya,* Calcutta Sanskrit Series, III, 1934, p. 17, śloka 28; 45, 18; 46, 26; 65. 17.

2. The two MSS. belong to the reign of king Harivarmadeva of Nepal and are dated Samvat 39.

3. I have stated above that *Mṛtyuvañcana* cannot at present be definitely identified; but some *Mṛtyuvañcana* texts are quite well-known in Tibetan Buddhist literature. The latest concordance of Tibetan Buddhist canons *(A Complete Catalogue of the Tibetan Buddhist Canons: Bkaḥ-ḥgyur and Bstan-ḥgyur;* published by the Tōhoku Imperial University, Japan, 1934) contains Tibetan translations of at least four such texts. They are: 1) *Ḥchibslu-baḥi sgrol-maḥi sgrub-thabs (Mṛtyuvañcanatārāsādhana),* no. 3495, also

Tantric; so are Mahākālacakra texts. The relation between Buddhist and Kālacakra ritual will be evident from the following passage in the *Laghukālacakratantrarāja-ṭīkā:*

> *Tasmād idānīṃ ratnatrayaśaraṇam gatvā kālacakratantra rāje laukikalokottarasiddhi sādhana mārgābhiṣekādhyeṣṇāṁ kurmaḥ*
>
> *Sakalasattvānaṁ samyaksambuddhattvalābhāya ihaiva janmanīti.*

These Tantric texts must have been prevalent among certain sections of the Buddhists of Upper Burma; and when we remember that the inscription refers to conditions in the fifteenth century when Theravāda Buddhism in Upper Burma had been on the ascendant for four centuries, the existence of Mahāyāna and Tantric texts in a monastic library seems at least to show that at one time these cults must have gained some popularity in the country.

The reference to Kālacakra texts is endowed with a better significance when we find Tāranātha, the celebrated Tibetan monk-scholar recording as follows:

> "Although in the countries of the Koki realm [in which the kingdoms of Pagan and Pegu are included] Vinaya, Abhidhamma and *Mahāyāna works* are very well-known, the secret *mantras* had become very rare *with the exception of Kālacakra,* the three *māla* sections and a few other".

The Taungdwin inscription and Tāranātha are thus found to agree which each other; indeed Tāranātha's statement, to which scholarly

---

translated in Chinese; 2) *Ḥchi bslu-ba sgrol-ma dkar-moḥi sgrub-thabs (Mṛtyuuañcana sitatārāsādhana),* no. 3496, also translated in Chinese; 3) *Ḥchi bslu-baḥi man-ring-gi sgrol-maḥi sgrub-thabs (Mṛtyuuañcanopadeśatārāsādha na),* no. 3504, also translated into Chinese; and 4) *Ḥchi-ba bslu-baḥi man-ṅag (Mṛtyuvañcanopadeśa),* no. 1748, also translated into Chinese. The translation from the Sanskrit original of the last one, into Tibetan, was made by the well-known Dīpaṅkara Śrījñāna with the help of his Tibetan collaborator, Rinchen bzaṅ-po.

The two Rattamālā (Raktamālā) texts cannot also be definitely identified, though the concordance referred to above mentions such Tantric texts as *Raktayamāritantrarāja* (no. 474) and *Raktayamārisādhana* (cf. nos. 2010, 2023. 2026, 2031, 2035, 3281, 3375, 3627) and similar others.

But I have some doubts as to the correctness of the two titles as we find them in the inscription. Can they be *Ratnamālā* and *Ratnamālā-ṭīkā* and not *Rattamālā* and *Rattamālā-ṭīkā?* Tantric Ratnamālā texts are well-known, and in the concordance referred to above, we have mention of several Ratnamālā texts (Cf. nos. 389, 2384, 2048, 3901).

scepticism attaches little value, is now confirmed by the actual existence of Mahāyāna and Kālacakra texts in Burma[1].

1. Tāranātha's fuller account of Buddhism in Burma will be dealt with in a subsequent chapter.

3
Gods and Goddesses of Northern Buddhism

We now come to more definite evidences of Mahāyāna Buddhism and allied cults in Burma. They are afforded by a considerable number of images in stone and bronze acquired from the ruins mainly of Hmawza and Pagan as well as by numerous paintings on the walls of the temples of Pagan depicting what can be identified as Mahāyāna and Mahāyānist Tantric divinities. The number of Such finds, it is true, is not as large as it is in Java or Kamboja, or in any other Indianised countries of South-East Asia, nor are the finds so representative of the pantheon. In fact, so far as can be determined at present, we meet with Avalokiteśvara, Maitreya, Tārā, Mañjuśrī, Lokanātha who is but another form of Avalokiteśvara, Hayagriva, Vajrasattva, and one or two other minor deities, for example, Jambhala, and a small group of Tantric gods and goddesses mainly recognisable by their significant attitudes in pairs. Among these Lokanātha seems to have been a very popular deity, a fact which we notice also in Kamboja, with Avalokiteśvara and Maitreya closely following. The images are mostly small; and a few of them had probably been imported, but on most of them the local stamp is evident. As to the paintings on the walls of temples, their testimony leaves no doubt; they are the one positive proof of the existence, in the heart of the Burmese capital, of a considerable number of Buddhists following the Mahāyāna and its allied cults. Even the imported images are significant, for, there would have been no necessity for their importation if no one wanted them. What is interesting in this connection is that a very large number of these sculptures, and almost the whole group of paintings may stylistically be dated after the introduction of the Theravāda by Anawrahta in 1057 A.D.; consequently the Mahāyāna and its allied cults were important factors in the religious life of Pagan even after the great Theravāda revival which the local chronicles extol. Burmese chronicles and inscriptions, it is true, ignore its existence; only in a few instances do they allude to the existence of a heterodox sect as a disturbing element in the religious life of the people.

Avalokiteśvara

Single images of Avalokiteśvara are very rare in Burma; in fact only about half-a-dozen definitely identifiable, have been brought to light. One is preserved in the Ānanda Museum, Pagan, and another has been recovered from the ruins of Hmawza. The former is a small bronze image standing in a slight *tribhaṅga* pose with the right hand in *varada-mudrā,* and the left holding a lotus-stalk. In front of the crown we notice the seated figure of Amitābha with his hands resting on his lap[1]. The second example, also from Hmawza, is a well executed bronze which on account of its style may be ascribed to the 7th or 8th century A.D. The god is shown standing in the *tribhaṅga* pose; of his four arms the two on the left are completely gone; one of the hands on the right was probably in the *abhaya-mudrā,* the other holds some unrecognisable object. But the high mitre-like head-dress with the figurine of Amitābha leaves no doubt as to the identity of the image[2]. Two more images which may be identified as two different forms of Avalokiteśvara are also known from Hmawza. One is a small standing image of bronze very badly damaged; the portion below the waist is missing; the left fore-arm and the entire right arm have gone. The image is richly adorned with ornaments, including a high *mukuṭa*[3]. Any definite identifiction mark is absent, and though we can not be certain if it represents Avalokiteśvara, there is no doubt that here we have an image of a Bodhisattva But the six-handed image made of thin gold plate and recovered from the Yindaik-kwin excavations is definitely identifiable as one of the various forms of Avalokiteśvara. The god is seated in *lalitāsana,* two of his hands are in the *vitarka-or vyākhyāna-mudrā,* and the remaining ones carry respectively a lotus with a stalk, a *caurī,* a trident and an indistinct object which may be a noose

1. *An. R.A.S.B.*, 1916, p. 3.
2. *An. R.A.S.I.*, 1911-12, pl. LXVIII, fig. 6.
3. *Ibid.*, 1928-29, p. 105.

or a rosary[1]. According to the *Sādhanamālā* there are as many as six varieties of the six-handed forms of Avalokiteśvara, *viz.*, Khaṣarpaṇa, Halāhala, Harihariharivāhanodbhava Lokeśvara and Sukhāvatī Lokeśvara[2]. But the present image does not exactly conform to the *dhyānas* attributed to any of them. Of these six Khaṣarpaṇa and Sukhāvatī Lokeśvara are seated in *lalitāsana*, the one point in which the present image agrees with the *dhyānas*.

Maitreya

Maitreya is the only Bodhisattva worshipped in Burma both by Hīnayānists and Mahāyānists; his worship seems to have been very popular. In Burmese inscriptions he is frequently mentioned as Metteyya, the Pālī form of his name; the supreme wish of the founder of a pagoda or other religious edifices, and the donors of lands, or books or other monastic necessities is 'to behold Metteyya', as in the Shwekugyi inscription of king Alaungsithu, or 'to obtain salvation in the presence of the Lord Buddha Mettañ', as in the inscription of the Lady Acawkrwam, daughter of Trilocandranāma Mahādevi Suṁlūlā, queen of Jayasura. Bodhisattva Maitreya also figures in a few Pāli-Sanskrit inscriptions on votive tablets of king Anawrahta and other important personages of Pagan. Here is an example:

Mayāniruddha-devena kṛtam, tena Maitreya-sambodho
labheyan nivṛtto [?] padam.

> By me, [king] Aniruddhadeva, [this mould of Sugata] has been made; through this [good deed] may I obtain the path of Nirvāṇa, when Maitreya is fully enlightened (i.e., when Bodhisattva Maitreya will have become a Buddha).

Maitreya is also mentioned in certain short Talaing inscriptions written on the walls of some of the temples of Pagan, along with Lokeśvara or Avalokiteśvara. The image of Maitreya in a monastic garb, very similar to that of Gautama, is still very common in Burma.

One or two single images of Maitreya are also known in Burma. The ruins of Pagan have yielded a small but beautiful bronze image

---

1. *An R.A.S.I.*, 1928-29, P. 105.
2. *J.B.R.S.*, 1912, II, I, p. 101

of Maitreya; it bears a mutilated inscription in Pyu of which the syllables *ba : Metriya: ba* can still be read. *Ba* : in Pyu is an honorific used with respect to kings and *devas*, and Metriya is evidently Maitreya; the inscription must refer to the image on which it is engraved.

The Mahāmuni image of Arakan, a gilt image of huge proportions possibly represents Maitreya; at least there are two early Burmese chronicles, the *Mahārāja Van Tawari* (vol. I, p. 209) and the *Pagan Rājā Van Thit* (MS. no. 918 of the Bernard Free Library, Rangoon), which state that it is an image of Maitreya[1].

Avalokiteśvara and Maitreya

In Burma as elsewhere these two Bodhisattvas are often placed on both sides of the Buddha as his attendants or *caurī*-bearers. In fact, examples of stone reliefs with similar representations are so numerous, both from Hmawza and Pagan, that they can hardly have exclusively belonged to the Mahāyāna. In some instances these reliefs form an integral part of the decoration of temples belonging to the Theravāda. Evidently both Avalokiteśvara and Maitreya were adopted, no doubt as subordinate deities, in the Theravāda pantheon (if Theravāda can be said at all to have a pantheon) of Burma, in the same manner as Indra and Brahmā of the Brahmanical pantheon were in the early Hīnayāna.

At Hmawza a piece of stone sculpture was found in which a standing Buddha figure is flanked by two *caurī*-bearers decked with elaborate ornaments and each crowned with a *mukuṭa*[2]. These attendants may be safely identified as Maitreya and Avalokiteśvara, in accordance with local traditions. The excavations at Yathemyo, a locality in Old Prome, yielded in 1910 a votive tablet[3] on the obverse of which "is the figure of the Buddha with an aureoled head. On his right is a small *stūpa*, and on his left is an object which looks like a flower. The pose of the Buddha is quite unorthodox according to Burmese ideas, and appears to be like that of Avalokiteśvara. The palms of both hands rest on the knees, and the

1. *An. R.A.S.B.*, 1909, p. 10.
2. *Ibid.*, 1910, P. 13.
3. *An. R.A.S.I.*, 1927-28, p. 125. pl. LIV, a.

right foot hangs down . . . On the proper right of the Buddha is a legend in Sanskrit ... The reverse face is divided into two panels. On the upper the Buddha is depicted in a sitting attitude, and is flanked by two Bodhisattvas. All the three figures have aureoled heads. The upper portion of the central figure is flanked by a *stūpa* and a lotus flower supported by its stalk which is apparently held by each Bodhisattva . . . On the lower panel is represented the Buddha in a sitting attitude with both hands outstretched. He is flanked by two female figures, each carrying a lotus-flower in either hand. The female on the left side of the Buddha is better dressed than the one on the right. She wears a long mantle which is divided in front and exposes a part of the bosom. The two panels are divided by a line in Sanskrit legend". As I could not trace the tablet among the finds of Old Prome, it was impossible to verify the identification of the Buddha figure on the obverse as Avalokiteśvara or of those two figures flanking the Buddha on the reverse face. Obviously they are creations of the Northern School of Buddhism, as is proved by the two Sanskrit legends, not yet published, on the two faces of the tablet. The two female figures holding lotus stalks are also significant.

The Pagan excavations of 1927-28 yielded a small bronze tablet representing three figures each of which is seated on a lotus-throne and is surmounted by a *stūpa*. The central figure, that of the Buddha, is seated cross-legged and is flanked on the two sides by two seated figures. The one on the right is seated cross-legged with his right hand in *bhūmisparśa-mudrā* and the left placed on the lap holding probably an alms bowl. The figure on the left is seated in *lalitāsana* with the right hand hanging down over the right knee, and the left resting on the corresponding knee. The two figures undoubtedly represent Maitreya and Avalokiteśvara.

In the same year a terracotta votive tablet was also recovered from the same site representing a similar triad: the Buddha between Maitreya and Avalokiteśvara[1].

Another stone sculpture representing the Buddha flanked by the same Bodhisattvas was recovered from the Sudaungpyi Monastery, Twante[2]. The Buddha is seated with his right hand in *abhaya-mudrā*

1. *An. R.A.S.B.*, 1915, p. 17.
2. *Ibid.*, f.n.

and his left in *varada-mudrā*. The lotus stamps them definitely as Bodhisattvas, but it is uncertain whether they are Avalokiteśvara and Mañjuśrī flanking the Buddha Dīpaṅkara, or Avalokiteśvara and Maitreya flanking the Buddha Gotama[1].

In a niche of the Ānanda temple, there is a relief showing a standing Buddha flanked by two figures with elaborate ornaments and a *mukuṭa*. Such groups are frequent in Burma, and it is tempting to identify these ornamented and crowned attending figures as Avalokiteśvara and Maitreya. Such terracotta votive tablets and stone reliefs are in certain instances inscribed with Sanskrit legends which are invariably in Eastern Nāgarī script. This also seems to connect them with Northern Buddhism[2].

Pagan has yielded a bronze stele representing the Buddha seated in *bhūmisparśa-mudrā* on a lotus-throne and flanked by two Bodhisattvas, evidently Avalokiteśvara and Maitreya. Both of them are seated in *lalitāsana,* a favourite attitude for Bodhisattvas. Both of these attendants hold a lotus with a long stalk in their left hand, while the right is in *varada-mudrā*. The pedestal of the throne shows in relief two gazelles seated face to face on both sides of the *dharmacakra;* the subject thus refers undoubtedly to the famous event in the Deer Park of Benares. The head of the Buddha is surrounded by an aureole schematically arranged in a decorative lotus design, and the round stele is finished with flame designs at the sides, and with a foliated design at the top. It is significant that the two figures are ornamented and crowned.

Tārā

A few images of Tārā are also known from Burma. A small bronze image of the goddess has been found near Manawgon village in Myothit township of the Magwe district. She is seated crosslegged on a lotus throne with her right hand in *varada-mudrā* and her left which is in *vitarka-mudrā* holds the stalk of a lotus-flower. She wears anklets, bracelets, armlets, a necklace, earrings and a crown. Her hair is arranged in a knot on the back of her head[3].

---

1. For a similar tablet see, *An.* R.A.S.I., 1927-28, pl. LV, fig. 2, p. 130..
2. *An. R.A.S.B.*, 1919, pp. 31-32.
3. *Ibid.*, 1916, p. 3.

Another image of Tārā which is now preserved in the Ānanda Museum, Pagan, can be easily recognized by her attitude[1].

The excavations at Hmawza have also yielded a small terracotta tablet representing an image of Tārā standing in a graceful *tribhaṅga* attitude, the four hands hold indistinct objects. A Sanskrit line in Nāgarī script runs around the image[2]. The style of the tablet suggests importation from Sārnāth or Nālandā with which places ancient Prome was in intimate contact during the 8th-10th centuries. On account of the style the tablet may be assizned to the 9th century.

Mañjuśrī

At least one image of Mañjuśri is known to us. In the Ānanda Museum, Pagan, which is a repository of a good number of important finds, there is a stone sculpture representing the well-known figure of the Bodhisattva Mañjuśrī seated in the *vajraparyaṅkāsana*. His right hand holds the sword which he sways over his head to dispel the darkness of ignorance; the left hand which generally holds the book of knowledge is unfortunately broken. His curly hair finishes at the top in a pointed *stūpa*[3]. The characteristics of the image conform roughly to the *sādhana* describing the Arpacana variety of Mañjuśrī. As many as eight *sādhanas* in the *Sādhanamālā* are devoted to the description of this variety. He is always described as seated in the *vajraparyaṅka* attitude, clasping the sword in his right hand, and applying the *Prajñāpāramitā* book against his chest, in the left. He is sometimes accompanied by four minor divinities: Keśinī, Upakeśini, Candraprabhā and Sūryaprabhā, and the four *Dhyānī-Buddhas:* Vairocana, Ratnasambhava, Amitābha and Amoghasiddhi. The present image is, however, represented single, and may be compared with an almost identical image in bronze from Nepal which instead of holding the book in front of the chest, clasps the stalk of a lotus on which the book is placed[4].

1. *An. R.A.S.I.*, 1927-28, p. 130, pl. LV. figs, 8a, 8b.
2. Ānanda Museum Exhibit no. V, 6, 2 ft. 6 in.
3. Bhattacharya, *Buddhist Iconography*, pp. 28-29.
4. *Ibid.*, pl. XVII, c.

Jambhala

Among the minor Mahāyāna deities Jambhala is in all probability represented by the remnants of an image recovered from the ruins of Hmawza. The excavations at the ancient city gate situated near the village of Kinmungyon yielded fragments of what was once a large-sized stone image. On account of the protruding abdomen and the elaborate ornaments, M. Duroiselle rightly identified it as Jambhala[1].

In the same spot were found fragments of terracotta tablets each of which bears a standing figure crowned with a *mukuṭa* and having four hands with some unrecognisable object in each. It may be assumed that they represent Bodhisattvas on account of their dress and ornaments as well as their attitudes. The ruins of Hmawza yielded in 1926-27, a large-sized stone sculpture (6′3″×4′2″×1′6″) which may definitely be identified as a Bodhisattva, though on account of the very damaged condition of the image and the absence of any distinctive mark, we cannot identify it more definitely. It wears a mitre-shaped headdress, wristlets and anklets, and is seated on a throne with the right knee raised and the left leg placed on a level with the throne, in an attitude resembling *rājalīlā*. The left hand rests on the left knee; the right is missing. The figure seems to be seated in a niche representing a temple, capped by a foliated arch which is adorned with flamboyant ornaments. In a panel below the throne are four guardians, two on each side of an object which looks like a salver; all are seated with one knee raised, and are holding in one hand the end of a club placed on the shoulder. Above, and flanking the Bodhisattva are two small crowned figures, probably representing royal devotees[2].

A fragment of a terracotta votive tablet representing a four-armed Bodhisattva is also known from Hmawza; but here too the absence of any significant attribute renders it difficult to identify the image. The god is seated in *lalitāsana;* one of the two left arms is broken off at the shoulder; the other, half of which has disappeared, rests on the left knee. The upper right hand is applied to the chest and holds an non-descript object; the other hangs down at the side. On the

---

1. *An. R.A.S.B.*, 1925, p. 16.
2. *An. R.A.S.I.*, 1926-27, p. 183.

right extremity of the pedestal is a kneeling figure in *namaskāramudrā*, and above it, a tiny *stūpa*. The connection of the image with the Northern School of Buddhism is further attested to by a short Sanskrit epigraph recording the Buddhist formula in Eastern Nāgarī script on the face of the pedestal[1].

Lokanātha

The Bodhisattva Lokanātha seems to have been more popular than other Mahāyāna deities which are only incidently known and were once worshipped in Burma; and his images are more numerous than those of any other god of the same pantheon. Thus, the Ānanda Museum, Pagan, shelters two bronze images of this Bodhisattva seated on lotus-throne. In each case the right hand is in the *varadamudrā*, and the left gracefully holds the stalk of a lotus-flower. On the right and left side there rise the stout stalk of lotus-flower in a delicate curve ending in flowers and foliage. Both figures are richly ornarmented with necklace, waistband, *karṇapūras*, armlets, wristlets, and anklets which are all elaborately, though not very delicately, moulded. Their heads are crowned with a *jaṭā-mukuṭa* consisting of long locks of curly hair. The iconographic features of these two images conform exactly to the *sādhanas* devoted to the Lokanātha variety of Avalokiteśvara. Of the four *sādhanas*, three represent him as single, and prescribe that the Bodhisattva should have two hands carrying the lotus in the left and exhibiting the *varadamudrā* in the right. He may sit in three attitudes according to the three different *sādhanas*, the *lalita*, the *paryaṅka*, and *ardhaparyarika*[2].

Besides the three *sādhanas* in which Lokanātha is represented alone, there is a fourth which describes him as accompanied by Tārā and Hayagrīva as well as by eight other gods, four goddesses and four *dvārapālas;* in fact the *sādhana* describes the whole *maṇḍala* of Lokanātha. The principal figure, white in colour, is described as two handed, the left holding a lotus and the right exhibiting *varada-mudrā*. "He sits in the *lalita* attitude … ., to his right is Tārā who has a peaceful appearance, exhibits the *varada-mudrā* and carries

1. *An R.A.S.I.*, 1926-27, pp. 182-83.
2. Bhattacharya, *Buddhist Iconography*, pp. 38-40. These images were up to now usually identified as Maitreya, which is evidently a mistake.

the lotus. To the left is Hayagrīva who exhibits the act of bowing and carries the staff in his two hands[1]. There exist representations of Lokanātha with attendant deities that do not exactly conform to the prescribed *sādhana*. Thus, we know at least two miniature paintings, both from Bengal, representing Lokanātha standing in the *ābhaṅga* pose with the left hand holding the stalk of a lotus and the right in *varada-mudrā*. One of them which is inscribed *Campitala Lokanātha Samataṭe ariṣasthāne* represents Tārā standing to his right with similar attributes, and Hayagrīva to his left. Two *vidyādharas* are represented in the sky on both sides of the head of Lokanātha[2]. The other example which is inscribed *Campita-Lokanātha-Bhaṭṭāraka* represents Tārā and Hayagrīva both seated in a graceful attitude, the former with his hands joined in prayer, and the latter holding the stalk of a lotus[3]. We know yet another inscribed miniature painting of Lokanātha, also from Bengal, in which he is represented as standing and six-handed. M. Foucher describes it as follows: "Bodhisattva white, standing with six arms; the right hands (1) in charity *[varada-mudrā]* (2) holding the lotus, (3) the rosary; the left hands (1) in charity, (2) indistinct object, (3) the book; four assistants: to the right, (1) a *preta* kneeling with a large belly, long beak-shaped mouth, here yellow, a green [female] Bodhisattva, *viz.*, Tārā. . . . On the left (1) red, (2) yellow with four hands (both Tārās)"[4]. The miniature is inscribed: *Harikeladeśe śila-Lokanātha;* therefore, there can be no doubt as to its being identical with Bodhisattva Lokanātha, though it does not, nor do the two described above, conform to the *sādhana* of the divinity.

On the left wall of the vestibule of the Kubaukkyi temple, Myinpagan, Pagan, there is a more than life-size painting of a divinity which from an iconographical point of view resembles the god represented on the miniature paintings of Bengal referred to above. The painting covers almost the entire wall, and the central position is occupied by a large-sized white-coloured figure, standing

1. Bhattacharya, *op.cit.*, pp. 38-39.
2. Cambridge Univ. MS. No, Add. 1643. For note and illus., see Bhattasali, *Buddhist and Brahmanical Sculptures in the Dacca Museum,* pp. 12-13, pl. I(a); Foucher, *Iconographie Bouddhique,* I, p. 102, pl. IV, 3.
3. A.S. Bengal MS. no. A 5. For notes and illus., see *ibid.*, p. 14, pl. II (b).
4. Foucher, *Iconographie Bouddhique,* I, pp. 105, 178, 200.

in a graceful *ābhaṅga* pose. But instead of six, he seems to have ten hands of which two are clasped as if in prayer to a superior divinity, in this case probably the Buddha himself who occupied the sanctum of the temple. Two hands hold long stalks of lotus-flowers and two others seem to be in *varada-mudrā.* The poses and attributes of the remaining hands cannot be made out. On both sides of the main figure two gods are apparently shown kneeling down with hands folded; and over the head we notice two three-headed figures, both seated on a *padmāsana* and holding lotus stalks in their hands. It is not unlikely that the two kneeling figures in prayer represent Tārā and Hayagrīva, for they here really occupy the position of subordinate deities. The two figures above possibly represent two of the eight attendant gods.

Reference to Lokanātha is made in at least two Talaing inscriptions painted on the walls of the Pagan temples. Two frescoes, one in the Cauk-hpaya-hla at Nyaung-u and another in a pagoda half a mile east of the Seinnyet Pagodas, are stated in contemporary handwriting to be pictures of Lokanātha. The Cauk-hpaya-hla fresco has evidently been disfigured, but the inscription below is clear. It has been read by Mr. Luce: *purhāloṅ Lokanat,* "the Bodhisattva Lokanātha". The latter, says Mr. Luce, "is a fairly large panel showing a standing Bodhisattva; it is unfortunately damaged in the centre, but he seems to be holding a lotus-bud in front of his chest". Mr. Luce does not say in which hand the god carries the lotus-bud, though, I presume, it must be in the left, while the right should be in *varada-mudrā;* if this is so, this example from Pagan agrees, as far as the main figure is concerned, with those of the miniatures from Bengal referred to above. The legend below the painting reads: *//O// īy kā purrhāloṅ' Loṅkanat te //O// īy kū lup so [ṅ]ā lha (s) aṅ (so) akluiw ra pā luiw sate lup klwañ so sa mliy kliy kywan kha [ps] im le ra pā ciy sate//.* This is the Bodhisattva Loṅkanat (Lokanātha). I, who made this cave-temple, desire to get a (fine?) reward. May I get sons, grandsons, slaves, a full set of them, also to support (me)".[1].

Vajrasattva

An image definitely belonging to Tantric Mahāyāna cult is

1. *J.B.R.S.*, XV, II, 1924, p. 141, f.n. 5.

preserved in the Ānanda Museum, Pagan. It is a stone sculpture representing a male and female figure embracing each other. Both figures are two-handed, the male being seated in the *vajraparyaṅkāsana*. This sculpture evidently represents a Mahāyāna deity with his *śakti* in the well-known *yab-yiom* position. The attributes in their hands are not clear, but it is permissable to identify the image tentatively as Vajrasattva who is the sixth *Dhyāni-Buddha*, and is regarded by the Vajrācāryas of Nepal as the priest of the group of the five *Dayānī-Buddhas*. When represented in *yab-yum,* he is closely associated with his *śakti* in embrace, and is represented as seated in *vajraparyaṅkāsana*[1].

Paya-Thon-Zu and Nandamañña Paintings: Tantric Gods and Goddesses

Among archaeological materials which are important in affording evidence of the existence of the Mahāyāna in Burma, we have now dealt with sculptures, bronzes and terracotta tablets, and a few examples of paintings representing Mahāyānist divinities. Incidentally we have mentioned inscriptions which confirm that evidence.

A still more fruitful source is provided by a long series of paintings found on the walls of a group of temples of Pagan. These paintings represent gods and goddesses that are evidently Tantric in character, and though it is not yet possible to identify them all with certainty, their affialition to the Tantric Mahāyānist pantheon is perfectly clear. It is curious that nearly all these paintings are found on the walls of temples at Min-nan-thu, a small village to the north-west of the main city of Pagan. Here we find the remains of a number of temples and monasteries the walls of which are covered with some of the best preserved frescoes in Burma, executed to serve the ends of a particular form of Buddhist worship, a sort of Mahāyānist Tantrism. Other localities in and around the ruined city of Pagan also abound in temples and monasteries containing such paintings, but their subject-matter, except in a few instances can hardly be described as Mahāyānist or Tantric. It seems therefore that Minnan-thu was the centre of the Tantric Mahāyānist sect which here had its monasteries and places of worship.

1. Bhattacharyya, *op. cit.* pp. 6-7, pl. IX, *c,d,e.*

It is not unlikely that after the introduction of Theravāda Buddhism into Pagan, and its subsequent official adoption by the State and the people, the adherents of these Northern Buddhist cults were obliged to withdraw from the heart of the city to the outskirts where in their own temples they continued to practise the ritual of their particular cult; this would explain why nearly, if not all, their pictorial relics are found in that one locality.

The most interesting group from our point of view consists of three small square temples together called the Paya-thon-zu, and the fourth, a few hundred yards from the Paya-thon-zu, called the Nandamañña. The three temples of the Paya-thon-zu each consist of a vaulted vestibule and vaulted corridors enclosing the four sides of a solid square structure of brickwork crowned by a *śikhara*. The three temples are joined by two narrow vaulted passages leading from the first to the second, and from the second to the third. On the walls of the eastern most of the three shrines there is a series of paintings representing Bodhisattvas embracing their respective *śaktis* Or Consorts. Some of them are shown holding a *śakti* in each arm; their dress is frankly secular, they wear coloured and printed skirts, elaborate ornaments and richly jewelled crowns, and their poses and attitudes are erotic and suggestive. Others are represented as seated with one *śakti* on one knee, or two, one seated on each knee. Some of the Bodhisattvas appear to have two hands only, but in several instances they have four and even six and eight hands holding different attributes and exhibiting various *mudrās*. I have not succeeded in tracing the *sādhanas* which would answer these Bodhisattvas with their *śaktis*, though the ideological relation is evident; in fact not one of these representations agrees in all details with any particular *sādhana* describing Bodhisattvas accompanied by their *śaktis*.

In one of the panels of the Paya-thon-zu, two exactly similar Bodhisattvas stand side by side in a slightly marked but graceful *ābhaṅga* pose. They wear the usual short skirt, ornaments and the richly decorated crown. Each of them has eight hands, two of which are held before the chest in what appears to be *dharmacakra* or *vyākhyāna-mudrā;* the remaining three on the left hold attributes just as the three on the right and these are what seem to be a flower (it resembles neither the lotus nor the *nāgakeśara*), the leaves of a palm-leaf book, and third, an indistinct object which may either be a shield or a rosary. Two figures kneel on two sides in the attitude of adoration. The whole panel is very interesting from an iconographical point of view, but our present knowledge of the pantheon of Northern Buddhism does not allow us to identify them. In this temple also, there is one figure with three faces, seated in *paryaṅkāsana* and provided with four hands holding attributes that are hardly recognisable. This figure may tentatively be identified with a variety of Maitreya, or with either of the two varieties of Mañjuśri, Nāmasaṅgīti and Mañjukumāra[1].

The central temple of the Paya-thon-zu group also has on its walls a fresco representing a seated Bodhisattva embracing two *śaktis* on two sides. It is a striking feature of these frescoes which was first pointed out by M. Duroiselle, that, whereas a few of these Bodhisattvas have unmistakable Burmese features, the *śaktis* they embrace are unmistakably Indian[2].

In the same group of temples there are several representations of a two-handed divinity standing in graceful *tribhaṅga* attitude with one of his hands, either the right or the left (in accordance with his position to the right or left of the main image in the niche), in *vyākhyāna-mudrā,* and the other clasping the stalk of a *nāgakeśara(?)* creeper. He is decked with elaborate ornaments from head to foot, and is dressed in a beautiful garment that flows from his loins to his ankles[3]. That he represents a Bodhisattva is certain, but one can hardly be more sure about his identification.

On one of the walls of the eastern-most temple of the Paya-thon-zu triad, to the right of a large niche, now empty, there is a vertical panel containing three separate rectangles representing different subjects[4]. The top-most and the lowermost rectangles each represent a Bodhisattva standing in a *tribhaṅga* pose, with two *śaktis* clinging on two sides, an oft-repeated scene in the Paya-thon-zu and Nanda-mañña Temples. The rectangle at the middle represents however a very interesting divinity standing in a slight *ābhaṅga* attitude.

1. Bhattacharrya, *op. cit.,* pls. XIIIb, XIVA, XVIc.
2. *An. R.A.S.B.,* 1916, pp. 12-13.
3. *Cf.* Arch. Sur. Burma, photo-negative no. 60/3207 (1929-30), 31/2234 (1921-22).
4. *Cf.* Arch. Sur. Burma, photo-negative no. 31/2234 (1921-22).

Besides his usual wealth of princely decorations and garments, he is endowed with ten hands, two of which are clasped in adoration in front of his chest, evidently in respect to the deity in the sanctum. The attributes in his eight other hands cannot unfortunately be recognized. Two figures, presumably females, squat with folded hands, on his two sides. No known *sādhana* of Buddhist iconography seem to agree exactly to its description, though it is evident that the deity must belong to the rich pantheon of the Vajrayāna. This is all the more significant, for it shows how little we know of the numerous gods and goddesses of this pantheon from written texts.

The paintings on the walls of the Nandamañña represent similar subjects, and are in some instances characterised by a much more sensual attitude. A large panel is exclusively devoted to the representation of a group of women in most voluptuous poses. An inscription set up within the precincts of the Nandamañña itself throws welcome light on the debased kind of Buddhism which these paintings serve to illustrate. Its purport is that the Nandamañña temple was built at the instance of King Narapatisithu, a devoted Theravādī and the founder of the celebrated Shwekugyi and the Thatbiññyu Temples, in 610 Sakkaraja (= 1248 A.D.), and it also refers to the monks who lived close by in a monastery, the remains of which can still be seen not very far from the temple itself. It further states that out of the revenues of the land dedicated to the temple the monks residing in the monastery were daily provided, morning and evening, with *meat*, rice, betel and *a jar of spirits*. Taking food in the evening, partaking of meat, and drinking spirit were particularly abhorrent to the Theravādīs which these monks certainly were not. Such practices of daily life seem rather to connect them with one of those later forms of Northern Buddhism which were largely influenced by Tantric rituals and practices, and the paintings seem to confirm that assumption. But what is even more curious is the fact recorded in the same inscription that Narapatisithu asked one of his ministers to build this temple and the monastery attached to it, and that he sent Shin Arahan, the Theravādī primate of the realm and the man who had brought the Theravāda to Pagan, to Tennasserim to bring a sacred relic to be deposited in the temple which evidently was associated with a Tantric cult of the Mahāyānists. This is an unique example of the spirit of toleration that existed at that time in the great metropolis of Burma, or shall we say, of the ecclectism of the Buddhism of Pagan which, though decidedly Theravāda, was largely moulded and reshaped not only by the primitive *nāga* and spirit worship but also by Viṣṇuite Brahmanism. It is not surprising that this new religion in trying to absorb the already existing Mahāyānist and Tantric cults would attempt compromises here and there, and in that process be itself influenced by them. But to this aspect of the problem we shall turn at the end of our study. In any case, these temples and the paintings on their walls, but most of all, the inscription of the year 1248 refered to above, prove not only that the Theravāda flourished in Pagan side by side with these Mahāyānist and Tantric cults, but also that the latter had considerable hold on the people and the court. The support and patronage of Narapatisithu and the primate Shin Arahan, both devout Theravādīs, are significant.

We have already stressed the fact that the Nandamañña is iconographically much more interesting than the Paya-thon-zu. The divinities pictured on its rich walls are much more erotic, and Tantric in character, and represents a greater variety. Besides the paintings described above, we have a number of representations of a divinity standing alone (without accompanied by his *śaktis*), richly jewelled, with one of his hands in *vyākhyāna-* or *abhayamudrā*, and the other clasping the stalk of a flower-creeper[1]. This divinity, evidently a Bodhisattva, is not definitely identifiable. But there is one representation of a god in one of the vertical panels which seem to lend itself to a more or less definite identification. The panel is vertical and is divided into three rectangles; in the topmost one, the Buddha in *vyākhyāna-mudrā* is represented as seated in *vajraparyaṅkāsana* discoursing to his two disciples seated on two sides. The middle rectangle presumably represents the well-known episode of the subjection of the Nālagiri elephant. The lowermost rectangle shows a divinity seated in what resembles the *ardhaparyaṅka* or *mahārājalīlā* attitude with his left hand in the *vitarka-mudrā,* and the right hand raised upwards holding the stalk of a flower-creeper. A winged *kinnara* with folded hands seems to

1. *Cf.* Arch. Sur. Burma, photo-negative no. 26/2229 (1921-22); 23/2226 (1921-22).

wait upon him to the right. No *sādhana* seems to agree with its description, but one may tentatively identify it with either Mahārājalīlā Mañjuśrī or Lokanātha[1]. There is almost exactly a similar representation in a corresponding panel on the other side of the particular niche of the temple[2].

Thanbula and Abeyadana Temples: Avalokiteśvara: Mañjuśrī: Lokanātha

Besides the Paya-thon-zu and the Nandamañaa which were evidently favourite resorts of the followers of the Mahāyāna and other allied cults, there still stand in the midst of the ruins of Pagan several other temples which bear testimony to the once prevailing Mahāyāna and its allied cults. I have already mentioned one or two such temples, but there are others still; notable among them are the Thanbula and the Abeyadana. On a wall of the eastern porch of the Thanbula Temple[3], Minnanthu, there is a painting representing a divinity seated cross-legged in an *ābhaṅga* position[4]. He is richly decked with ornaments and is crowned with a conical *mukuṭa* with flamboyant designs. His right hand is in *vitarka-mudrā* and the left is in what may be called *varada-Mudrā.* Floral creepers flourish in delightful curves on both his sides. The representation does not easily lend itself to an identification, though one readily recognizes here a Bodhisattva, perhaps Avalokiteśvara. On a wall of the temple at the south-east corner of a field near the Somingyi Pagoda, Myinpagan, there is a representation of a standing Bodhisattva, almost exactly similar in decorative and iconographical details to those we have already noticed on the walls of the Paya-thon-zu and the Nandamañña[5]. Artistically a better representation of the same divinity can be seen in a painting on a wall of another little known temple[6] in Pagan. The attitudes and *mudrās* of the

1. *cf.* Arch. Sur. Burma, *op.cit.*, no. 24/2227 (1921-22).
2. *Ibid.*, no. 82/3229 (1929-30).
3. Said to have been built in A.D. 1255, by Thanbula, queen of Uzana, king of Pagan. *Amended List of Ancient Monuments in Burma,* 1921, p. 28.
4. Arch. Sur. Burma, photo-negative no. 19/3286 (1930-31).
5. *Ibid.*, no. 63/3480 (1931-32).
6. Unfortunately, I could not get the name of this temple; it does not seem to have been recorded in the list of the Archaeological Survey of Burma.

hands slightly differ in the present case[1]; but it may not be very wrong to identify all similar paintings as representing Avalokiteśvara who seems to have been the most popular Bodhisattva in Burma. It is not also unlikely that they may also be identified with either Maitreya or Mañjuśrī. The positions they occupy on the walls have some significance in this respect. Each wall is generally provided with a deep niche at the centre which must have once sheltered a stone or brick image of the Buddha; in fact, in several instances these images can still be seen occupying their respective places. On the outer wall of the two sides of the niche are to be seen two large paintings representing, as described above, two standing divinities in almost identical attitudes, with similar dress and ornaments. That one of them is Avalokiteśvara, and the other Maitreya or Mañjuśrī, there can be no doubt; but it is not easy to see which one represents Avalokiteśvara and which one Maitreya or Mañjuśrī. There is nothing in their attitudes or in their attributes to distinguish them.

A most interesting temple is the Abeyadana[2], at Myinpagan. In the niches disposed around the walls of the corridor of this temple one can still see some beautiful stone images of the Buddha seated in conventional *mudrās;* on its walls there are remarkable examples of paintings, some of the very best we find in Burma, representing Buddhist subjects in which gods and goddesses of Northern Buddhism predominate, and what is no less interesting, also depicting some Brahmanical deities among whom at least two are recognisable at once[3]. Built by Kyanzittha, son of king Anawrahta

1. Arch. Sur. Burma, photo-negative no. 147/3414 (1930-31).
2. Said to have been built by king Kyanzittha (c. A.D. 1084), son of Anawrahta.
3. As these materials were not available to me when my *Brahmanical Gods in Burma* was published (1932), I take this opportunity to identify these two paintings here. One of them (Arch. Sur. Burma, photo-negative no. 6/3423 of 1931-32) represents Śiva riding on his bull Nandī. In his two hands he carries the *damaru* and the *triśūla*; round his neck hangs the snakegarland, and from his *jaṭā-mukuṭa* flows the sacred stream of the Gaṅgā. The other (Arch. Sur. Burma, photo-negative no. 40/3307 of 1930-31) represents the goddess Yamunā riding her favourite *vāhana*, the tortoise, that holds in its mouth what seems to be a full-blown lotus-flower. The goddess is endowed with four hands of which two are held together in front

who introduced Theravāda Buddhism in Upper Burma, and himself the builder of the sublime Ānanda, that abiding monument of the Theravāda faith, the Abeyadana is perhaps one significant example which represents the eclectic nature of the religious life of contemporary Pagan, combining in one not only Brahmanism and Buddhism but also the two apparently conflicting creeds of the latter faith. This temple along with a number of others, definitely prove that the Mahāyāna which must have preceded the Theravāda, at least in Pagan, was still a living religion with a considerable section of the population, though the latter came to be established as the official religion of the State[1].

---

of her chest with palms exposed, and two others hold non-descript objects. A standing figure, presumably a female, and provided with a halo, seems to follow her. So far as I know, this is the only representation of this goddess fron Burma.

1. It is interesting to note that the paintings of the Abeyadana (11th century) and similar other temples, not unoften containing representations of gods and goddesses of Northern Buddhism, e.g. the Kubyaukkyi (11th cent.) of Myinpagan, the Nagayon (11th cent.), the Patothamya (11th cent.), are executed in a style which is more akin to the classical Indian style represented in the almost contemporary manuscript paintings of Bengal; while the paintings of the Paya-thon-zu (13th cent.), the Nandamañña (13th cent.), the Thanbula (13th cent.) etc. seem to owe their affiliation to the somewhat later tradition of Nepalese paintings as well as that of Jain manuscript paintings of Western India. It is equally interesting that a few of the former group of temples contain Talaing writings, a fact to which my attention was drawn by Prof. G. H. Luce of the University of Rangoon. A further Comparison of the ground plans and other architectural features shows that, as in their paintings, so in their architectural style, they fall into two different groups, the former (which is also earlier in date, majority of them belonging to the 11th century) I would prefer to designate as the "Indo Burmese" type, and the latter (which is also later in date) as the "Burmese type" of which one of the earliest specimens is the Shwekugyi (12th cent.), and one of the best the Thatbiññyu (12th cent.). The Ānanda (11th cent.) perhaps represents the stage of transition. Some models of the "Indo-Burmese" type can be seen represented on some manuscript paintings from Bengal and on some stone reliefs from the same place. The Shwezigon, the Shwesandaw, the Mingalazedi etc. belong entirely to a different class which, in the long Tun, proved to be the most popular architectural form in Burma. To my opinion, the Sliwezigon type belongs to the same tradition of architecture as does the Barabuḍur of Java. But this is not the place to go into details about the architecture of Pagan which I reserve for a Inext monograph now in course of preparation; here I have taken the opportunity to

Coming back to the paintings themselves from the Abeyadana, we find one interesting horizontal panel on the east wall of the east corridor of the temple representing a divinity seated in *Lalitāsana* with a graceful *ābhaṅga*. His right hand is shown in *varadamudrā* and the left in what resembles the *vyākhyāna* attitude. A full-blown lotus-flower rises in a delightful curve at the left, and two female attendants kneel in adoration on two sides[1]. The *āsana,* the *mudrā* and the lotus-flower seem to indicate that the god represented is Lokanātha who, we have already seen, was a popular Bodhisattva in Burma.

In the same temple, on the western portion of the south-wall there is an exquisite drawing consisting of two empty niches, one above the other[2]. The upper niche is flanked by two standing figures who are evidently attendant deities or simply *dvārapālas* attending on the divinity, presumably the Buddha, supposed to occupy the niche. The figure on the right holds in his right hand a round wheel, and in his left a pointed sword raised up to the corresponding shoulder; that on the left holds a spear in his right hand and a round wheel in his left. Both are crowned and elegantly decked with ornaments, and on both sides of each rise stalks withhalf-blown and full-blown lotuses. It is difficult to offer any identification for these two persons, but if they are attendant deities, they certainly represent Bodhisattvas.

Intervening the two niches there is a horizontal panel which depicts six different scenes, short but dramatic. I can offer no identification of any of them, but one of them, the third from the right, representing an ascetic seated in *vajraparyaṅkāsana,* with a garland of skulls round his neck and carrying a female figure on his shoulders, seem to represent a Tantric ritual.

---

make known a logical classification of the bewildering monuments of Pagan, I record with thanks the suggestions I received from Prof. G. H. Luce in this connection.

1. Arch. Sur. Burma, photo-negative no. 32/3299 of 1930-31.
2. Ibid, no. 9/3426 of 1931-32. This is one of the best preserved drawings from Pagan. No attempt at any study of these drawings and paintings of Pagan from their artistic stand-point and as to their place in the history of Indian painting is made here. For such a study, readers are referred to my *Indo-Burmese Art. Part I. Sculptures, Bronzes and Paintings.*

The niche at the bottom is also guarded by two divinities, seated in what resembles the *ardhaparyaṅkāsana*. Both are crowned and wear usual ornaments. The one on the right carries a shield in his right hand and a spear in his left; the other holds the *cakra* in his right hand and the sword in his left. But what is most interesting, both of them appear to wear what seem to be skin boots. From his attributes (e.g., the *cakra* and the sword) and the boots, the figure on the left may perhaps be identified as that of Sūrya, but in that case the seated position is somewhat unusual. The figure on the right does not seem to reveal its identity, if it is not taken as Aruṇa, the charioteer of Sūrya; but, it is safer to know them at present simply as attendant deities.

Just above these two figures there are depicted two divinities seated in *lalitāsana* on two full-blown lotus-seats and each flanked by two kneeling worshippers. The right hand of the figure on the right is in *varada-mudrā* and the left clasps the stalk of a lotus-flower that blossoms just above the corresponding shoulders. The hands of the figure on the left are in exactly similar positions, but on the full-blown lotus-flower we can easily notice the *Prajñāpāramitā* book. The two figures perhaps respectively represent Avalokiteśvara and Mañjuśrī.

On the east wall of the east corridor of the same temple is represented a god seated in *ardhaparyaṅkāsana* with his right hand holding a rosary *(akṣamālā)* and his left clasping the rod of a long trident resting diagonally against his body[1]. The figure does lend itself to an identification, not but it certainly belongs to the varied pantheon of the Vajrayāna.

Hayagrīva

On the same wall there is a painting depicting another interesting god of the Vajrayāna pantheon. He is represented as seated in *ardhyaparyaṅkāsana,* and carrying a *vajra* in his left hand raised above the corresponding shoulder. The attribute in his right hand cannot unfortunately be determined. The god is painted in red colour, and what is still more significant is that over his crown peeps out the head of a horse[2]. The painting can at once be identified

1. Arch. Sur. Burma, photo-negative no. 30/3297 of 1930-31.
2. *Ibid.*, photo-negative no. 31/3298 of 1930-31.

as depicting Saptaśatika Hayagrīva. The *sādhana* lays down that Hayagrīva when depicted as an independent deity has red colour, carries the *vajra* and the *daṇḍa* in his two hands and shows the horse's head over his crown[1]. The painting agrees wonderfully well with the *sādhana*, and we can assume that the right hand of the god carries the *daṇḍa*. So far as I know, this is the first image of Hayagrīva that has up to now been recognized in Burma.

---

1. Bhattacharyya, *Buddhist Iconography*, pp. 53-54.

4
The Ari Sect and The Samaṇakuṭṭakas: Tantric Buddhism in Burma

Who Were The Aris?

The wall-paintings of the Paya-thon-zu and Nandamañña Temples, as we have seen, and the evidence of the Tibetan monk scholar Tāranātha (as will be shown in a subsequent chapter) point to the existence of a Tantric Buddhist sect in Pagan, and perhaps also in other localities in Burma. This sect was probably that of the Aris (who, in my opinion, were the same as the Samaṇakuṭṭakas, referred to in the *Sāsanavaṁsa*) who, according to Burmese tradition, had their principal centre on the Popa hill at Thamahti near Pagan where their cult persisted, inspite of repeated royal persecutions, till probably as late as the closing decades of the eighteenth century. Much has been written about the Aris and their cult; quite a number of scholars have attempted to throw light on the history of this mysterious sect, and whatever has been recorded of them in traditions, local chronicles and inscriptions has been discussed at length[1]; their identity has long puzzled scholars until M. Duroiselle gave a most comprehensive account[2] discussing all evidences at his disposal, and identifying the Aris as a sect affiliated to the Northern School of Buddhism and fully saturated with Tantrism,

1. Phayre, *History of Burma*, p. 3: Hüber, *B.E.F.E.O.*, 1909, p. 584: Finot, *J.A.*, 1912, p. 121; Taw Sein Ko, *Burmese Sketches;* Duroiselle, *J.B.R.S.*, 1911, I, i, p. 126; Harvey, *History of Burma*, pp. 17-18, 60, 95, 313; but the *locus classicus* is certainly Duroiselle, *An. R.A.S.I.*, 1915-16, pp. 79-93 ("The Aris of Burma and Tantric Buddhism"). Since Duroiselle wrote, more about the Aris have become known, as a result of our better knowledge of the local chronicles, e.g. the *Hmannan*, and of the wall-paintings of Pagan. This chapter attempts a more up to date account based on all the facts so far known.
2. *Op. cit.*

All evidences tend to support M. Duroiselle's conclusions. Here we wish only to present the subject in a fuller and more correct historical perspective than lay within the scope of M. Duroiselle's study, and stress those points which lend support to his conclusions.

Among the sources relating to the Aris and their cult, the information supplied in the *Hmannan* is the most detailed and interesting: it will be necessary to give a full account so far as possible of the source materials in this connection before attempting any interpretation. No apology will be needed if we proceed to quote entire extracts from the *Hmannan* dealing with the Aris and their cult. This will, we shall presently see, help us in explaining and corelating other references to the sect from different sources, including such as do not mention them by name.

Extracts from The Hmannan

a. Now the farmer became king [Nyaung Sawrahan, 931-964 A.D.] and was great in glory and power. At his cucumber plantation he made a large and pleasant garden, and he wrought and kept a great image of Nāga. He thought it good thus to make and worship the image of Nāga[2], because Nāga was nobler than men and his power greater. Moreover, he consulted the heretical[3] Ari monks regarding the Zigon.

---

1. "Ari is the phonetic transcription of the name; it is written Arañ; following the written form, Hüber *(B.E.F.E.O.*, 1909, p. 584) derives this word from Araññaka, basing himself on the Thai inscription of Rame Khombeng at Sukhotaya, in which the word Āraññaka occurs, and which he took to be the same as the Burmese 'Ari' in its full form. But M. Finot *(op. cit.)* has shown that Āraññaka is a proper name, that of a monastery in a forest. Pāli words ending in *ññ (a)* are never abbreviated in Burmese, but always retain their pure form. Moreover, the Aris were not ascetics living in forests, like the Buddhist and Brahmanical Āraññakas, but lived together in large monasteries in, or on the skirts of, villages. The word Ari comes from Ārya, (noble); Pāli final *y(a)* becoming in Burmese regularly *ñ*, which is always pronounced i. Duroiselle, *op. cit.*, p. 92, f.n. 2.
2. Here one can see how the pre-Theravāda Buddhism of Pagan was permeated by Nāga Worship, which continued to have its share of influence even after the Theravāda reformation.
3. Note that these adjectives are used by the author or authors of the *Hmannan* who were admittedly Theravādīs of a much later date. Note also the attitude, in these extracts, how the later and more orthodox Buddhists held this earlier heterodox sect in disrespect, if not in positive contempt, and how they loved to narrate the story of the attempts made to root them out.

pagodas in the Kingdom of Yathepyi and Thaton, and he built five pagodas: Pahtogyi, Pahtonge, Pathothamya, Thinlinpahto and Seitto-pahto. In them *he set up what were neither spirit images nor images of the Lord, and worshipped them with offerings of rice, curry and fermented drinks, night and morning*. Since the root beginning made by Ashin Punna the elder in the life time of the Lord Omniscient, throughout the reigns of the dynasties of the Burmese kingdoms of Tagaung, Tharakittara, Arimaddana and Thiripyissaya, there flourished the *paramattha* order, the *samuti* order, the sacred writings, their study and intuition. But *afterwards the religion gradually grew weak from the reign of king Thaittaing, founder of the city of Tampavati, and because there was no piṭaka or sacred writ, only the doctrines of the Ari Lords at Thamahti were generally adopted, and in the reign of king Sawrahan the king and the whole country held these doctrines*[1].

b. Seeing that *the people had been fondly clinging to the doctrine of the Ari lords for thirty generations of kings of Pagan*, Anawrahtaminsaw (Anawrahta, 1017-1053] filled with virtue and wisdom, *rejected the rank heresies of the Ari lords* and followed the precepts of Shin Arahan, known as Dhammadassi. Whereupon those Ari lords in order that the people might believe that doctrine, made manuscripts to suit their purpose, and placed them inside a *thahkut* tree; and when the *thakut* tree became covered with scales and bark they sought and seduced fit interpretors of dreams and made them read and publish the manuscripts found in the *thahkut* tree. So that the king and all the people misbelieved[2].

c. In the reign of Anawrahtaminsaw the kingdom (of Arimaddanapura) was known as Pugarama [another name for Pugāmā or Pagan]. Now *the kings in that country for many generations had been confirmed in false opinions following the doctrines of the thirty Ari lords and their sixty thousand disciples* who practised piety in Thamati. It was the fashion of these Ari monks to reject the Law preached by the Lord and to form each severally their own opinions. They wrote books after their own heart and beguiled others into the snare. According to the Law they preached, a man might take the life of another and evade the course of *karma* if he recited the formula of depreciation *(paritta)*. Such false and lawless doctrine they preached as the true doctrine. Moreover, *kings and ministers, great and small, rich man and common people, whenever they celebrated the marriage of their children were constrained to send them to these teachers at nightfall, sending as it was called, the flower of their virginity*. Nor Could they be married till they were set free early in the morning. *This sending of the flower of virginity means an act of worship. Hence scholars connect in meaning this 'sending to the monastery to worship'*

1. Maung Tin and Luce, *Glass Palace Chronicle*, pp. 59-60.
2. *Ibid*., p. 39.

with the word 'viharamaho'. And scholars in their stone inscriptions use this phrase, 'the time of the first sending to the monastery'.

But Anawrahtaminsaw was a king of ripe perfections, and when he heard and saw these wrong lawless doings he was displeased, knowing thern for false doctrine. And he yearned vehemently to discover the true Law[1].

d. The noble saint *Dhammadassi* [i.e., Shin Aharan] *having come to Pagan ministered to the religion. When the king and all the people forsook their on opinions and were established in the good Law, the Ari lords lost their gain and honour and bore great hatred against Shin Arahan.* And the king fearing that the Ari would practise ill against him, took good heed and appointed guards enough to defeat the thirty Ari lords and their sixty thousand disciples. At that time there came many saints and counsellors of those who were faithful in the religion. And the king unfrocked the thirty Ari lords and their sixty thousand followers and enrolled them among his spearmen and lancers and elephant-dung sweepers. And the king said: *"Our royal grandsires and great grandsires who ruled this kingdom in unbroken line, followed the doctrine of the Ari monks.* If it were good to follow them again, I would fain follow them". So fain was he, it is said[2].

The extracts above quoted do not allow us to decide at what time the cult of the Aris was introduced in Pagan[3]; but it is clear that already before the middle of the tenth century, they were so powerful that the king and the whole country held their doctrines. And even without taking the number of thirty Ari lords or their sixty thousand disciples too literally, we may assume that they counted numerous followers and were an important factor to be reckoned with when Anawrahta made the first attempt to curb their influence. They had their centre at Thamahti, a village not very far from the Pagan metropolis, and after the introduction of Theravāda Buddhism Anawrahta conducted a relentless perse-cution

1. Maung Tin and Luce, *op.cit.*, pp. 70-71.
2. *Ibid.*, pp. 74-75.
3. Extract (b) purports to say that the people had been clinging to the Ari doctrine for thirty generations of kings at Pagan. Number 30 and its multiples, with Burmese chroniclers, seem to have had a traditional significance. However, the present statement is evidently an exaggeration and an well-known old method of hinting at hoary antiquity. But there is no reason to disbelieve the statement in extract (d) that the "royal grandsires and great grandsires of king Anawrahta. had followed the doctrine of the Ari monks".

against them. What is self-evident in these extracts is that even the *Hmannan* which was compiled at the court of a king subscribing to the purer faith of the Theravāda, by scholars who had been zealous followers of the faith, and at a time when the whole country had long been under the profound influence of Ceylonese Buddhism, even that *Hmannan* does not state or imply that the Aris were not Buddhists. Its implication is rather to the contrary, for it says that they were monks, living in monasteries, and what is significant, they believed in the recitation of the *paritta.* According to the *Hmannan* their doctrines were false, evidently because they widely diverged from those of the purer faith which the authors of the *Hmannan* professed and which their people had professed for centuries.

Old faiths die hard. Anawrahta's Crusade against the Aris was only partially successful; their power, it is true, was broken to a great extent, but they were not extirpated. In a Burmese inscription which may be dated in the latter half of the twelfth or the early part of the thirteenth century[1], a specific mention of the Aris occurs not long after the events referred to above. It says:

> "One thousand bowls filled with cooked rice were offered to the *Arañ.* A silver Buddha was also given for the Arañs to worship. My son became a monk and listened to the first sermon. A gold Buddha was made. At the time when my son received ordination and listened to the first sermon, slaves, cattle and property were given".

The *Arañ* of the inscription doubtless refers to the Aris who continued to receive new adepts, as this record seems to prove, even as late as the date of the inscription.

Another definite mention of the Aris occurs in connection with Thihathu's son Sawyun (1315 A.D.; Sawyun was ruler of Saggaing) who enlisted some Aris among his armed retainers[2]. It may be recalled that Anawrahta also enrolled some of the Aris among his spearmen and lancers. The *descendants of the Aris* (Ari-gyi-do-ahnwe) seem to have been numerous at Pinya, Ava and Saggaing, and were even patronised by kings. "They were so called owing to their love of sports, especially boxing of which they gave public

1. Insc. no. 176 in the *List of Inscriptions found in Burma,* Archaeological Survey, Burma, 1921.
2. *Hmannan,* VI.

exhibitions. They set all monastic rules at nought, were great drinkers, and had a weakness for another sex; they kept their hair about two inches long, wore a kind of cylindrical hat, and robes of a colour not orthodox; they dabbed in alchemy and popular medicine; they sold amulets and recipes for the attainment of magical power; and they bred, rode and sold horses and exercised themselves in the use of arms. They were powerful at Ava in the fifteenth century, in the reign of king Pathama-min-gaung; the chiefs among them had free entrance of the palace at any time of the day, and there, it is said, they often drank so immoderately as to be sent back to their monasteries in palanquins. They are still mentioned in the eighteenth century when a thousand of them suddenly sailed from Ava and put to flight a party of Talaings, with whom the Burmese were often at war"[1].

It is evident that the original doctrines of the Aris had undergone a complete transformation and the sect existed in a degenerate condition without having any religious hold or significance. The later descendants of the Aris were only known as such, but they had very little to connect themselves with those from whom they claimed to have been descended.

Who Were The Samaṇakuṭṭakas?

Besides the specific references to the Aris and their descendants we meet with certain references in inscriptions and chronicles which may, in the light of the extracts already quoted from the *Hmannan,*

---

1. Duroiselle, *op. cit.*, pp. 92-93. Elsewhere in his very illuminating article, he says: "Anawrahta's persecution had the unexpected result of spreading the sect in remote parts of Burma, and its remnants, though not styled Ari, are still existent among a large number of Shan monks, among whom the original doctrine has been forgotten, though the characteristic laxity of morals has persisted. Amongst the Burmese themselves, at the Burmese capitals and other places of some importance, a degenerate form of Ari may be said to have lasted well into the 18th century; the manuscripts of the Ari seem to have disappeared as well as the right to the *jus primae noctis*, the animal sacrifices, and the easy doctrine about the remission of sins; but the spirit of the old sect survived in the love of good cheer, copious drinking and women. The greatest part of this transformation is no doubt due to the great religious reformation of Buddhism carried out in the fifteenth century by king Dhammaceti, as recorded in the Kalyāṇi inscriptions", *op. cit.*, pp. 91-92.

be interpreted to refer to the self-same sect, though no definite mention of them is made.

The *Sāsanavaṁsa* refers to a heretic sect, that of the Samaṇakuṭṭakas who are said to have gained a footing in Pagan at a very early period; they existed there, we are told, from the time of Samuti, and "continued to grow and multiply till in the time of Anuruddha (Anawrahta) the adherents of the Samaṇakuṭṭakas numbered many thousands. The chief and most dangerous heresy is briefly described; it lies in the boundless abuse of the *paritta* which becomes, with these heretics a charm to absolve from guilt even the murder of father or mother. Such doctrines (together with others that raised the ācariyas to tyrannical power over the family of the laity) had corrupted the religion of Tambadvīpa[1], when in the eleventh century a new era opened with the arrival of the great thera Arhanta, from Thaton"[2].

It is unnecessary to go into details and point out parallelisms to show that the Samaṇakuṭṭakas of the *Sāsanavaṁsa* were the same as the Aris of the *Hmannan.* The two accounts read side by side Teveal at once that the latter says exactly the same about the Aris as the *Sāsanavaṁsa* tells us about the Samaṇakuṭṭakas. But the most interesting and conclusive parallelism is furnished by a further comparison of the Samaṇakuṭṭaka heresy with the Ari priest's claim to what is called in the *Hmannan* 'the flower of virginity'[3]. This is suggested by the following sentence in the *Sāsanavaṁsa* in connection with the Samaṇakuṭṭakas:

> "*Sace pi putradhītānaṁ āvāhavivāhakammam kattekāmo bhaveyya ācariyānam paṭhamaṁ niyyādetya āvāhavivāhakammam kattabbam; ye idam carittaṁ atikameyya bahu apuññam pasaveyyā ti*"[4].

If any one wishes to give sons or daughters in marriage, he must

1. An inscription of the seventeenth century, quoted by Burmese diplomats in negotiation with the British Government and translated for his Government by Col. Burney who was resident at Ava, 1837, places Pagan, Ava, Pinya and Myingyan in Tambadvīpa. Yule, *Mission to the Court of Ava,* p. 357. The *British Burma Gazetteer*, however, identifies Tambadvīpa with the upper portion of the Thayet district on the east bank of the Irrawady (vol. II, p. 746).
2. Bode, *Sāsanavaṁsa*, pp. 15-17.
3. As for the wide prevalence of this and similar custorm see, Pelliot, *B.E.F.E.O.*, 1902, p. 127; Duroiselle, *op. cit.*, pp. 88-89.
4. *Sāsanavaṁsa*, p. 16.

first hand them over to the *ācariyas* before giving them in marriage: whosoever transgresses this rule commits great sin[1].

Besides this specific references to the Aris and Samaṇakuṭṭakas, there is at least one other reference that almost certainly relates to this heterdox sect. It is in the Nandamañña inscription of 1248 A.D., already mentioned in a preceding chapter where its significance has been pointed out. Here is the relevant passage from the inscription:

> "The minister commanded that these things be dedicated to the monks . . . two potfuls of rice, two baslcets of betel-nut (and) betel-leaf, one and a quarter viss of meat, one ten-quart pot of long-fermented liquor. . . . This offering was made in the presence of my lord the king"[2]

Doubtless it indicates Ari survivals as late as the middle of the thirteenth century, and even under so pious a king as Kyawsa. The actual word 'Ari' does not occur in the inscription; but considering that the locality has always been described as the home of the Ari, the erotic and Tantric character of the paintings of the temple itself and the mention of meat and spirits to be provided for the monks, there cannot be the least doubt that this temple and the attached monastery along with others of the locality (e.g., the Paya-thon-zu group) were homes of the mysterious sect of the Aris. "The very omission of their name further shows that the Ari were then recognized as a long standing and matter of fact institution; further more, the building of monasteries and temples and the providing of more than the usual necessaries of monkish life for their use, is a proof that, far from having been exterminated by king Anawrahta in 1057, as we are told, they were held, on the contrary, in high esteem, not only among the people, but also at the court"[3].

Some Additional Arguments

The moot point to be decided in this connection is whether the Aris were really a Buddhist sect. Opinions have very naturally

---

1. This point has also been stressed by Dr. Mabel Bode, *op. cit.*
2. *Inscriptions of Pagan, Pinya and Ava*, 1892, no. 251; for the date and other historical implications, *see, An. R.A.S.B.*, 1919, pp. 22-23.
3. Duroiselle, *op. cit.*

differed on this question. Mr. Phayre contended that they were not Buddhists in any sense of the term[1], while M. Finot held that Viṣṇu was the god of the Aris[2], and that their cult was purely a primitive and indigenous one influenced largely by Nāga worship. M. Hüber and Mr. Taw Sein Ko opined that they represented a debased form of Mahāyāna Buddhism influenced by the indigenous Nāga cult on the one hand and Śivaism and Tantrism on the other[3]. The most considered opinion was put forward by M. Duroiselle according to whom the Aris were a Buddhist sect belonging to the Northern School, "ministering to the superstitions of the people, and were priests of the Nāga and spirit worship than prevalent in the land, and officiated at the bloody sacrifices connected with this indigenous worship. About the eighth century the wery profoundly influenced by Tantricism and were addicted to grossly immoral practices owing to *śākta* influences generally, and perhaps more particularly to intercourse with the followers of Vajrayāna and Sahajiyā cults of Bengal and Nepal"[4].

It is unnecessary to go over the same ground as M. Duroiselle has done; he has discussed the question from all points of view, and readers are referred to his article. I would here point only to two or three aspects of the evidence at our disposal that go to support his conclusions.

It has already been pointed out that the extracts quoted from the *Hmannan* seem to own the Aris as a Buddhist sect, but they were considered heretics because they had deviated from their original faith and had thus weakened their own religion. The implication of the *Hmannan* appears also to be supported by the *Sāsana-vaṁsa* which as we have seen styles the Aris as Samaṇakuṭṭakas or "false samaṇas" who corrupted the original religion by their boundless abuse of the *paritta*. If it means anything, it seems to suggest that these Samaṇakuṭṭakas were in reality Buddhist monks, but were gradually so degenerated owing to a number of causes that they were considered heretics by the followers of the Theravāda. Among the contributory causes may have been the primitive

1. Phayre, *History of Burma,* p. 33.

2. Finot, *op. cit.*, pp. 125-126.

3. Hüber, *B.E.F.E.O.*, 1909, p. 584; Taw Sein Ko, *Burmese Sketches,* p. 179.

4. Duroiselle, *op. cit.*, p. 93.

practise of *jus primae noctis,* bloody sacrifices and the drinking of liquor associated with it, and not a little the onrushing tide of Tantric Buddhism from Bengal.

But more definite evidences are afforded by the paintings of the Paya-thon-zu and Nandamañña temples and the Nandamañña inscription of 1248. The two temples were evidently Buddhist places of worship; the main figure enshrined in the sanctum in each temple is that of the Buddha seated in the *bhūmisparśa-mudrā* and on the walls and ceilings of each are painted numerous figures of Buddhas and Bodhisattvas. One of the frescoes of the Nandamañña represents a standing figure of the Bodhisattva Avalokiteśvara with his right hand in the *varada-mudrā,* and accompanied on the left by his *śakti* Tārā. This and similar other representations of Bodhisattvas prove definitely that these temples were Buddhist places of worship affiliated to the Mahāyāna and its allied cults. The Nandamañña inscription is also another definite evidence on this point.

Had the temple not been intended as a place of Buddhist worship, there could hardly have been any necessity for the long and arduous journey that Shin Arahan was asked to undertake to fetch a Buddha relic from Tennasserim to be deposited in the temple.

Last of all there is the Burmese inscription no. 176, already referred to[1], which definitely connects the Aris with Buddhist worship and typically Buddhist ritual. Images of the Buddha were made and other rituals were performed on the occasion of the ordination as a monk of a lay man who subsequently listened to the first sermon, and thus joined the rank of the Aris.

---

1. *List of Inscriptions found in Burma,* Archaeological Survey, Burma, 1921,

5
Testimony of Buddhist Monks

Accounts left by Buddhist monks throw a flood of light on the history of Buddhism in the Indianised countries of South-East Asia including Burma. Most useful from our point of view is the wellknown history of Buddhism by the Tibetan monk Tāranātha, and an account of travel by his *guru* Buddhagupta, a Buddhist monk. Their testimony appears to have been summarized in a Tibetan work of a somewhat later date, the *Pag Sam Jon Zang*. But Tāranātha supplies the fullest account; we shall therefore begin with his account and take Buddhagupta next. As the *Pag Sam Jon Zang* mostly draws upon Tāranātha, it is unnecessary to dwell on the evidence it contains. We need only state how far it confirms Tāranātha with regard to our subject. Moreover, its account is far too short[1].

Tāranātha and His Account

The introduction of Mahāyāna Buddhism in Pagan, Pegu and Arakan was already a thing of the past when Tāranātha wrote his celebrated history. It is unfortunate that the attitude of modern historians in dealing with the valuable account of this honest and concientious chronicler of the events of his religion has always been one of exaggerated scepticism. In matters of chronology and as a connected history, and with regards to names of kings and princes, his account is no doubt at great variance with that of more reliable records; but when he is recording chips of historical or geographical information, especially in connection with the history of his own faith nearer his own times, he gives us on the whole very important information on historical events although dressed some-

1. Das, *Pag Sam Jon Zang*, pp. 123-24.

times in fantastic garb. He thus enables us to fill up gaps in our knowledge of the history of the period, and to explain otherwise uncountable facts and factors.

Whoever studies the account of the monk-historian must admire in him an attitude approaching that of a modern historian, as far as it was possible in his days, for, he cared to give an account, though short, of the sources and source-materials from which he drew materials of his work, in the last chapter of his work[1]. A good number of historical texts he rejected as unreliable; he largely depends on Kṣemendrabhadras work in 2000 *ślokas* wich was supplemented by Indradatta's *Buddhapurāṇa* and Bhaṭaghati's[2] history of the succession of the *ācāryas*. Besides these, the *Mañjuśrīmūlakalpa*, a text belonging to about the 8th century, and now widely known among scholars, is also known to have been one of the important sources utilised by Tāranātha. For the history of Aparāntaka, Kashmir, Udyāna, Tukhāra and the Koki land, our monk-historian frankly confesses to have had no authority to draw upon. A remarkable evidence of his honesty is that when he draws upon merely on tradition he puts on record that he does so, and when he has neither tradition or earlier extant works to refer to, he is frank enough to say, "I have not heard", or "I have no earlier work of history", and he leaves his readers to draw their own inferences. One may therefore safely use Tāranātha's account to his advantage so long as it does not contradict known facts or factors of history, and to the extent they may be said to supply information not only upholding but also explaining the logic and circumnstances of already established facts.

It has long been known to scholars that Tāranātha's history of Buddhism in India refers to the introduction of the Mahāyāna and its allied cults in Burma, more particualarly in Pagan, during the rule of the Senas of Bengal. But the implication of this reference has hardly been properly understood, nor has Tāranātha's account presented in its true perspective. It is therefore proposed to give

1. Schiefner, *Tāranātha's Geschichte des Buddhismus in Indien*, St. Petersburg, 1869.
2. Bhaṭaghaṭi perhaps is *Bhaṭṭaghaṭi*, a class of Brahmin paṇḍitas. *Cf. Bandyaghatis* of Bengal who are well-known in the province, and are often alluded to in nineteenth century Bengali literature.

here relevant extracts in full from Tāranātha, so that the whole account as far as it relates to the history of Buddhism in Burma may be understood in its proper setting[1].

Extracts from Tāranātha

A

Chapter XV. Events of the time when the venerable Nāgārjuna was the guardian of the Creed[2]

". . . . In the east, in Paṭaveṣa or Pukam[3] and in Oḍiviṣa, Bhangala[4] and Rāḍha many temples were erected. At this time in Magadha, the Brāhmaṇa Suviṣṇu erected 108 temples, and 108 schools of *Abhidharma* teaching in order that the *Abhidharma* of the Mahāyāna and the Hinayāna does not decline. Towards the end of his life, the venerable Nāgārjuna went to the regions of the South[5], and after he has converted the king Udayana he defended the creed for many years . . .".

B

Chap. XXIV. Events of the time of king Śila (Śri Harṣa Śilāditya][6]

". . . Jayadeva also was a great ācārya who was learned in many sacred texts, and lived in Nālandā for a very long time. I have received no detailed biography of him. At this time a tooth of the Buddha reached Hasam[7] in the north. The poet Guhyadatta, a pupil of *ācārya*

1. The following extracts in English, it must be mentioned, are not from original Tibetan, but from Schiefner's German; but whenever and wherever I had doubts, I consulted the Tibetan text and satisfied myself as to the Correctness or otherwise of the German translation. It is a tribute to German scholarship that even at that early stage of Tibetan studies, Schiefner could follow the original so closely and so faithfully.
2. Schiefner, *op. cit.*, p. 72.
3. Paṭaveṣa is certainly Paṭaviṣaya, just as Oḍiviṣa is Oḍraviṣaya. It shows that Pukam or Pagan had another name, Paṭaviṣaya.
4. It is certainly Baṅgāla (= Vaṅga = roughly Eastern Bengal). *Cf.* Baṅgāla deśam of the Tirumalaya inscription of Rājendracola.
5. This is a faithful record of a well-known historical event, now more firmly established by the discovery of Buddhist remains at Nāgārjunikoṇḍa, a site that bears the name of Nāgārjuna.
6. Schiefner, *op. cit.*, p. 147.
7. Hasam = Asam = mod. Assam. At the time when Tāranātha wrote the pronunciation in Tibetan of what is transcribed in English by "h" was silent, so that Hasan is really Asam.

Saṁghadāsa, and Dharmadāsa's pupil Ratnamati offered a sacrifice together with a large body of followers amounting to many hundred thousands of people who lived according to the Law in the four classes(?). That tooth still exists at present in Pukhang[1]. . .",

C

Chap. XXXVII. Events of the time of the Four Senas and Others[2]

[According to Tāranātha, the first Sena king was Lavasena who was succeeded by his son Kāśasena. Kāśasena was succeeded by his son Manitasena, and the latter by his son Rathikasena. "Although the number of years", says Tāranātha, "for which every one of them reigned is not known, all four together they have not ruled more then about 80 years".]

". . . At the time of these Four Senas the Tirthas[3] increased more and more in Magadha, and there also appeared many followers of the Mleccha system of the Tājikas[4]. In Odantapurī and Vikramaśilā, the king erected a sort of fortress and a few soldiers were put into it for defending it[5]. In Vajrāsana (Bodh-gayā), a Mahāyāna school was

1. Pukhang = Pukām = Pukān = Pagan.
2. Schiefner, *op. cit.*, pp. 252 ff.
3. By the word "Tīrthas", Tāranātha, I think, meant the Brahmins whose influence during the rule of the Senas was admittedly on the increase.
4. The Tājikas must here refer to the followers of Islam. They are referred to in the Nausari grant (738-39) of the Lāṭa Cālukya prince Pulakeśī Avanijanāśraya, probably also in the *Vikramāṅkadevacaritam* of Bilhana, under the name of Taikas who under their leader Mahmud of Ghazni and his son Masud overran a considerable portion of Northern India during the period A.D. 1000-1037, and also by the Kāśmīrī chronicler Jonaraja.
5. This agrees on the whole with the account given in the *Tabaqāt-i-Nasirī* by Minhāj-ud-din (trans. by Raverty) of the description of the fortified city of Vihāra. Minhāj describes the city he captured as a "fortress', though, in fact, it was a Buddhist *vihāra* with a library and a college. It is common knowledge that at Odantapurī also, there was a large Buddhist establishment. The attack of Ikhtiyar-ud-din-Muhammad resulted in the capture of the 'fortress'. The capture is this described by Minhāj: "Muhammad-i-Bakhtyar, by the forces of his intrepidity, threw himself into the postern of the gateway of the palace, and they captured the fortress, and acquired great booty. The greater number of inhabitants of the place were Brāhmaṇas, and the whole of those Brāhmaṇas had their heads shaven, and they were all slain, [Evidently, the informants of Minhāj took the shaven headed Buddhist monks as Brāhmaṇas]. There were a great number of books there, and when all these books came under the observation of the Mussalmans they summoned a number of Hindus, that they might give them information respecting the import of these books; but the whole of the Hindus had been

founded, and there appeared also a few yogīs and Mahāyānists who preached the Law; during the summer sojourn there assembled 10,000 Saindhava Śrāvakas (Hīnayānists from Sindhudeśa); mostly *the other centres of learning declined.* It is said that in Vikramaśilā and Odantapurī, a great assembly came together which was of the size of the time of Abhayakara[1]. After the death of king Rathika wlien Lavasena was ruling, a few years passed in peace; after that in the land of Antarvedi between the Gaṅgā and the Yamunā appeared the Turuṣka king Candra through the intermediary of various bhikṣus who were messengers of the king: he combined himself with others in Bhangala and small princes of the Turuṣkas living in other regions and conquered the whole land of Magadha, killed many ecclesiastics in Odantapurī and destroyed this as well as Vikramaśilā[2]. On the site of the Odantavihāra a fortress of the Tājikas was founded. The Paṇḍita Śākyaśrī went to Jagaddala situated in Oḍiviṣa in the east. After he had stayed there for three years he came to Tibet; Ratnarakṣita, the senior, went to Nepal; the great savant Jñānakaragupta and the other great paṇḍitas went to the South of India with about hundred small paṇḍitas. The great savant Buddhamitra and Daśabala's pupil Vajraśtī and many other small paṇḍitas fled to the South. *The savant Saṅgama Śrījñāna, Raviśrībhadra, Candrakaragupta and the remaining sixteen mahāntas and 200 small paṇḍitas went farther to Pukham, Muñjan, Kamboja to the east, and other lands; in Magadha the Creed was almost extinguished. Although, at this*

killed. On becoming acquainted (with the contents) it was found that the whole of the fortress was a college, and in the Hindu tongue, they call a college, *vihār*". (Raverty, p. 552).

The account in the *Tabaqāt-i-Akbarī* by Nizām-ud-din is also substantially the same *(Bibliotheca Indica,* Trans. by B. Dey, p. 50). It is thus clear that what is described as the 'fort of Vihār', was really a fortified University town, and Tāranātha is therefore right when he says that at Odantavihāra the king erected a sort of fortress for defence against the oncoming invaders.

1. He is perhaps identical with Abhayakaragupta, the author of *Munimatālaṁkāra,* composed in the 13th year of the reign of king Rāmapāla of the Pāla dynasty of Bengal, See, Cordier, *Catalogue,* III. 314.
2. Tāranātha evidently refers to the invasion of 'Muner and Bihar' by Muhammad-i-Bakhtyar, but it is curious that he gives an Indian name, Candra, to the Turuṣka king. However, his account substantially agrees with that of Minhāj, quoted above. The story of the massacre of the monks and the destruction of the *vihāra* of Odantapurī is common to both. But that the Turuṣka, king was helped in his cause by various bhikṣus 'who were messengers of the king', and that he combined himself 'with others in Bhangala and small princes of the Turuṣkas living in other regions, are pieces of information which have often been ignored by historians, but which may not be without significance. Circumnstantially, both facts are not only possible, but also highly probable.

time there lived many magicians and people who cultivated magic there was no means of working miracles calculated to further the well-being of creatures. At this time the *yogīs* succeeding Gorakṣa were very simple-minded, and in order to attain honour from the Tīrtha kings[1] became Īśvara followers[2] in as much as they said that they too would not resist the Turuṣkas[3]. Only the small school of Nateśvara remained in the Buddha. Creed. Lavasena, his son Buddhasena, his son Haritasena, his son Pratītasena etc. were kings of very limited power, because they had to take order from Turuṣka kings . . . ".

D

Chap. XXXIX. Spread of the Creed in the Eastern Koki country[4]

" . . . Eastern India consists of three parts: Bhangala and Oḍiviṣa belong to Aparāntaka, and are called the eastern part of Aparāntaka. The north-eastern countries: Kāmarūpa, Tripurā [= Tipperah] and Hasam [= Assam] are called Girivarta, i.e. surrounded by hills. Going from there to the east to the side of the northern mountains are the Naṅgata lands, the land of Pukham [= Pukām = Pugāmā = Pagan] situated on the ocean, Balgu etc., the land of Rakhān [= Arakan), Haṁsāvatī [= Pegu] and other parts of the empire of Muñjan; further east Campa, Kamboja and others. All together are generally called Koki.

"In these Koki countries appeared from the time of king Aśoka sects of ecclesiastics[5], later in ever large numbers, and they became very numerous, but up to the time of Vasubandhu they were only Śrāvakas; after a few pupils of Vasubandhu had spread the Mahāyāna, it

---

1. i.e., Brahmin kings, i.e. the Senas.
2. Probably those who had been followers of the Gorakṣa cult came to be converted to the Brahmanical religion, a historical fact which is now recognized by scholars.
3. It is well-known that the Brahmins of the court of Lakṣmaṇasena advised the king not to resist the Turuṣka invader (*cf.* Raverty, *Tabaqāt-i-Nasirī*, pp. 555-56). After Muhammad-i-Bakhtyar had conquered Bihar, "a number of astrologers, wise men and counsellors of his kingdom", represented to Lakṣmaṇasena that it was written "in our books of the ancient Brāhmaṇas" that this country would be conquered by the Turks. They told him that the Muslim army had already conquered Bihar, and "next year they will surely come into this country". They therefore advised the king to "be removed from the country in order that we may be safe from the molestation of the Turks. The king did not however agree to leave the country, but most of the Brāhmaṇas and inhabitants of that place fled".
4. Schiefner, *op. cit.*, pp. 262-63.
5. *Cf.* the Sinhalese tradition of the Asoka mission of Soṇa and Uttara to Suvaṇṇabhūmi.

continued to exist almost uninterruptedly; from king Dharmapāla there were very many in Madhyadeśa who attained knowledge there; particularly at the time of the four Senas about half the ecclesiastics assembled in Magadha was from the Koki countries. And for this reason the Mahāyāna had spread very much; the Mahāyāna and Hīnayāna were not always distinguishable as in the Tibetan regions. From the time of Abhayakara the Mantrayāna spread more and more; at the time when Magadha was conquered by the Turuṣkas, the scholars of the Madhyadeśa came for the most part to that region and the creed was spread overy where. At that time lived the king Subhajāta; he erected many temples and founded about two hundred centres of teaching. When after him the king Siṁhajaṭi was come, and the latter raised the excellent creed still more in esteem than before, was the creed very much spread in all these countries, and when from time to time the ecclesiastics assembled, it is said that they number still at present about twenty to thirty thousand bhikṣus; there were also many upāsakas. . . Although in all these countries *Vinaya, Abhidhamma* and Mahāyāna works were very well-known, the secret *mantras* had become very rare with the exception of *Kālacakra*, the three māla sections and a few others. . . ".

E

Chap. XL. The manner of dissemination of the Creed on the small islands and the re-dissemination of the Creed in the South, etc.[1]

". . . Further in the Siṁhaladvīpa[2], Yavadvīpa[2], Tāmradvīpa[3], Suvarṇadvīpa[2], Dhanaśridvīpa[3], and Payigudvīpa[3], in these small

1. Schiefner, *op. cit.*, pp. 263-65.
2. They are evidently Ceylon, Java and Sumatra.
3. Tāmradvīpa is perhaps the same as Tāmraliṅgam of the Jaiya inscription of 1230, Madamaliṅgam of the Tanjore inscription of 1030, and Tan-mo-ling of Chau-ju-kua (1225). It was probably identical with the whole breadth of the Malaya Peninsula. For identification of Tāmraliṅgam = Madamaliṅgam = Tan-mo-ling, see, Coedès, *B.E.F.E.O.*, 1918, pp. 15-18. Compare, in this connection, Tāmrapattanaṃ mentioned in a Sanskrit Nāgarī inscription from Arakan (11th cent.) where Ānandacandra seems to have been the king. The context of the inscription seems to point to Arakan where we must try to locate Tāmrapattanam. One may also invite the attention of readers to a passage recorded by Chavannes *(Religieux Eminents*, p. 100*)*. Taolin, a Chinese pilgrim, "was tossed on ship-board over the seas of the South. He passed the "Pillars of Copper", and reached the country of Lang-chia. He crossed the kingdom of Ho-ling (Java), and traversed the country of the Naked People (Nikobar) . . . After several years he reached Eastern India in the kingdom of Tan-mo-li-ti (Tāmralipti) . . ." I have not unfortunately the Chinese for "Pillars of Copper", but I have suspicion that it stands for a region having a significant Sanskritic name connected with *tāmra* or

islands the creed was known from the earliest times and is very much spread even at the present day".

"In the Siṁhaladvīpa there are also partly followers of the Mahāyāna[1], but Śrāvakas are much more numerous, so that at present on the occasion of the Śrīpādukā festival, i.e. the festival of the foot prints, about 12,000 bhikṣus gather, most of whom are Śrāvakas. In Dhanaśri and Payigu there are also a few followers of the Mahāyāna, and in the other small islands there are only followers of the Śrāvakas. . . ".

I have on purpose given elaborate quotations from Tāranātha, and noticed in foot-notes points where the Tibetan chronicler finds

---

copper, and which may even be identical with Tāmraliṅgam of the Jaiya inscription. Taolin's route lends colour to that assumption. It is curoius, and attention to this was drawn for the first time by the late Prof. Sylvain Levi, that there were so many regions scattered on the three sides of the Bay of Bengal having a common generic name connected with the Sanskrit word *tāmra:* Tāmraparṇī (the island of Ceylon, and also the river of that name in the farthest south of the Indian continent), Tāmralipti (modern Tamluk in Lower Bengal), Tāmrapattanam (perhaps in Arakan), Tāmradvīpa, Tāmraliṅgam, and probably also "Pillars of Copper". Compare also in this connection: Suvarṇadvīpa (Sumatra) Suvaṇṇabhūmi (Thaton region of Burma), and similar names.

Dhanaśrīdvīpa: One is tempted to see in this name the Sanskrit form of Talaing Tanaṅsrī or Tnaṅsī (according to the Paklat edition of the *Upannahaṁsawatirājawaṁsakathā,* p. 140) = modern Tennasserim. The earliest Burmese form Tanaṅsari is found in the Nandamañña inscription of 1248 *(Inscriptions of Pagan, Pinya and Ava,* p. 250). In the Thūpārāma pagoda. inscription of Saggaing (1444), the form is Tanaṅsāri *(Inscriptions collected in Upper Burma,* 1900, p. 95: *Inscriptions copied from the stones collected by king Bodawpaya,* I, 1897, p. 225). See, Luce, *J.B.R.S.* XIV, ii, 1924, PP. 155-156 and f.n. 4.

Payigudvīpa is certainly Pegu: Payigu = Paigu = Pegu.

1. Among others, here is a point that upholds the general authenticity of the account of Tāranātha. With regard to Ceylon, Tāranātha states that the Sinhalese Buddhists were mainly Śrāvakas, but included some followers of the Mahāyāna. In this connection we may refer to the finds of a good number of Mahāyāna images in Ceylon, and quote the account of Hiuen Thsang who describes the Buddhist brethern of Ceylon as Mahāyānist Sthavira. "There came a time", the pilgrim continues, when "too much attention to peculiarities made two sects, the Hīnayānist school of those who belonged to the Mahāvihāra, and the school of those who belonged to Abhayagiri *and embraced both vehicles.* "The *Life* however describes the Buddhist brethern of Ceylon as Mahāyānists and Sthaviras, and *Fanchih* calls them simply Sthaviras (Watters, *Yuan Chwang,* II, pp. 234-235).

or seems to find support from independent sources. It will be seen that Tāranātha's account in general agrees remarkably with known facts. It not only does not contradict any of the established facts of history, but supplies us with a logical and coherent sequence of events that fit in satisfactorily within the already set frame. We may safely leave out extracts A and B, which deal with events that were far removed from Tāranātha's own time; moreover they have hardly any bearing on our present subject; but there is no reason to doubt the general trustworthiness of the extracts C, D and E, if, of course, one does not quarrel with the names of the Sena kings. I have pointed out in notes that the historicity of the account as given in these extracts, as far as they relate to events in Bihar and Bengal, and the geographical information contained in them are fairly correct. We need not, therefore, be sceptical regarding the general authenticity of Tāranātha's account of the introduction of the Mahāyāna and allied cults in Burma.

Tāranātha Summarised

Tāranātha includes Pukham (Pagan)[1], Rakhān (Arakan) and Hamsāvati (Pegu) in the Koki land[2] which also comprised the Naṅgata lands, Balgu etc., other parts of the empire of Muñjan (besides Haṁsāvati and Pegu)[3], and also Campa and Kamboja. According to the monk historian Buddhism had been introduced into these Koki countries as early as the time of Aśoka, gradually growing in importance thereafter. Until the time of Vasubandhu, it was the orthodox school that flourished most. Vasubandhu began his religious career in the school of the Sarvāstivādins, but was later

---

1. Pukham is described to have been situated on the ocean. This is not at all far from facts, for the Pagan empire during the Anawrahta dynasty did really extend to the shores of the sea in the south and west.
2. It is not improbable that the Koki land is the same as the tract of the country inhabited originally by the Kukis, a hill tribe of the frontiers of Assam, Arakan and Upper Burma. See, *Linguistic Surv. of India*, III iii, p. 2.
3. It is difficult to understand what Tāranātha exactly means by the empire of Muñjan in which he includes among others, Rakhān and Haṁsāvati. Pegu and North Arakan were definitely under the domination of Pagan during the rule of the Pagan dynasty. At present I am not in a position to identify Naṅgata lands and Balgu.

converted to the Mahāyāna (Watters, *Yuan Chwang*, I, pp. 357-358), and himself made a large number of converts in that faith. Some of his pupils are credited with having spread the Mahāyāna in the Koki countries, and from that time the Mahāyāna began to flourish there. In fact, the Koki land apparently became such an important centre of this faith that a good number of Buddhist monks of Madhyadeśa had 'attained knowledge' there; and later at the time of the 'Four Senas', about half the ecclesiastics of Magadha came from those countries. The Mantrayāna also is said to have spread there from the time of Abhayakara (10th cent.). At the time when Magadha was captured by the 'Turuṣkas' who had already destroyed the *vihāra* of Odantapurī and killed many ecclesiastics, a very large number of Buddhist scholars of the Madhyadeśa including Saṅgama Śrījñāna, Raviśrībhadra, Candrakaragupta, sixteen *mahāntas* and 200 small paṇḍitas fled to Pukharm, Muñjan, Kamboja and other countries; in Magadha Buddhism (evidently Tāranātha is always speaking of the Mahāyāna) practically became extinct. The Koki countries also supplied at a later period scholars to Tibet, among whom were Varnaratna and other paṇḍitas. Although in the countries of the Koki realm, '*Vinaya, Abhidharma* and Mahāyāna works were very well-known, the secret *mantras* had become very rare with the exception of *Kālacakra*, the three *māla* sections and a few others.' And not only in Pagan alone, but in Tennasserim and Pegu as well, there were a few followers of the Mahāyāna, though 'in the other small islands there were only followers of Śrāvakas'.

In Defence of Tāranātha

A scholar like M. Finot[1] has warned us not to be misled by the 'apparent precision' of Tāranātha's valuable account. Such warning is justified, since Tāranātha wrote a long time after the events which he narrates, and since he could not avail himself of any reliable authority on the religious history of the Koki land. We cannot expect of Tāranātha to produce an absolutely exact historical account of the subject he dealt with. His rōle was otherwise, and he was not also above or ahead of his times. But even admitting

1. *Op. cit., J.A.*, XX, 1912, p. 121 ff.

all this, we have seen that the account he furnishes is not very far from history, and the nearer he is to his age, the more reliable is his evidence which, in almost all the instances quoted above, except with regard to the names of Sena rulers, is in accordance with facts. I have already pointed out in notes where they corroborate facts already known and well-established, and one would readily find that in the main the evidence afforded by the monk-historian is more confirmatory than original. One may at once refer to his account of the Odantapurī and Vikramaśilā vihāras and of the invasions of the Turuṣka kings which are the same as found in other sources. In our extracts his evidence is rarely original or supplementary; but whenever this is the case, it is hardly ever in conflict with already known facts of history. The story of the introduction of Buddhism in the Koki land is an example. But, so far as our present knowledge goes regarding the subject as derived from other independent sources, mostly archaeological and literary, there is hardly anything to doubt in the general authenticity of Tāranātha's account. In fact, such a course of events as he speaks of is only in the logic of circumnstances, and satisfactorily explains the sequence that otherwise remains unexplained..

Tāranātha flourished in the sixteenth century, and when he wrote the tradition he recorded with regard to the propagation of Buddhism in the Koki land was still more or less within the memory of the people. His account generally confirms our conclusions from epigraphic, literary and other documents, mainly found at Pagan. Intercourse between Pagan and Hmawza on the one hand and Bengal and Bihar on the other from the eighth to the fourteenth century approximately is attested to by the discovery at Pagan and Hmawza of a large number of terracotta votive tablets with Sanskrit epigraphs in Eastern Nāgarī characters. To the same period, roughly speaking, belong also the numerous examples of art, in stone and bronze, which may stylistically be said to have been affiliated to the Eastern School of Art that had its home in the modern province of Bihar and Bengal[1], and flourished during the centuries covered by the Pālas and Senas to whon Tāranātha makes

1. See, *J.I.S.O.A.*, 1934, Ray, "Sculptures and Bronzes from Pagan":*Ind. Ant.*, LXI, 175-79, 197-200, Ray, "The Nathlaung Temple and its gods".

so significant a reference. The most convincing evidence is furnished by a number of Mahāyāna and Tantric deities themselves recovered from the *debris* of ruins that to-day cover the wide waste of. Pagan and the thinly populated village of Hmawza, a few inscriptions referring to certain Mahāyāna divinities, and an entire series of wall-paintings depicting gods and goddesses belonging definitely to the Mahāyāna and its allied cults. We have also seen the existence of a Buddhist sect grossly addicted to Tantric practices, and finally of Mahāyānist and Tantric Buddhist texts in a fifteenth century monastic library. Still more significant is the existence of *Kālacakra* texts to which Tāranātha makes a specific reference. All these are definite and independent proofs of the prevalence of the Mahāyāna and its allied cults in Burma of which our monk-scholar furnishes so vivid an account.

M. Finot also finds it puzzling to think how the Tibetan scholar could have ignored the grand religious reformation of the Theravāda in the eleventh century (under the active patronage of Anawrahta) which gradually developed into the official religion of the Pagan empire. But one must not forget the important fact that Tāranātha was chiefly concerned with Indian Buddhism and wrote his account more from the point of view of the introduction of the religion from India into the Koki land of which modern Burma is a part. He was, therefore, less interested in the vicissitudes of the religion in the Koki land itself. Tāranātha was a follower of the Mahāyāna and its allied cults, and during the period with which his present account is concerned, Buddhism of the Northern School was the prevalent religion of Eastern India. He was concerned with those later forms of Buddhism, so that he hardly cared to record what transformations the Hīnayāna had undergone in Burma. Moreover, in all probability he had never visited Burma, nor heard anything of the great religious reformation inaugurated by Anawrahta, which, however, had no more than a local significance. Tāranātha's account is not therefore to be relied upon to draw any straight conclusion as to the relative position of the two great schools of Buddhism in Burma.

We may therefore accept in a general way what Tāranātha says about the propagation of the Mahāyāna and its allied cults in Burma. In fact, M. Finot admits it when he says that his account is 'not exact so far as it affects Kamboja and Campa. The information of Tāranātha does not go beyond Burma'[1].

Biography of Buddhagupta

It has already been observed that in compiling his history of Buddhism in the Koki land Tāranātha had no earlier text or any other written document at his disposal to draw upon. But there is no reason to assume that he drew mainly from his imagination or depended merely on floating tradition. In fact, the very nature of his account reveals that he had at his disposal some reliable source which he drew upon in compiling his history. One such source has recently been brought to light through the admirable researches of Dr. Giuseppe Tucci[2].

This authority was an Indian Buddhist monk, named Buddhagupta, who was the spiritual teacher of Tāranātha[3]. Buddhagupta was a great traveller; he visited many places in India and Burma, the islands of the south-eastern seas, and even in Africa, with a view to find traces of Buddhism and of Buddhist remains. He also went to Tibet where Tāranātha met him and evidently heard from him the account of his travels and of the state of Buddhism in the countries he had visited. Tāranātha later on embodied it in a short biographical note called *Grub c'en Bu-ddha-gupthaḥi rnam t'ar rje brtsun ñid zal nas gzan du ran tog gi dri mas ma spags paḥi yi ge yan dag pa.* The importance of this note is chiefly geographical.

The life and travels of Buddhagupta have been incorporated in a biography written in Tibetan under the title *Sans rgyas sbas pa.*

It is important as a source of geographical information, regarding numerous places in India, Burma, Africa and several islands of the Archipelago. It, moreover, "shows that at the time of Buddhagupta

1. Finot, *op. cit.*
2. Tucci, "The sea and land travels of a Buddhist sādhu in the sixteenth century", *Ind. Hist. Quart.*, VII, iv, PP. 683-702.
3. The *Sam-bha-laḥi-lam-yig* of Blobzaṅ dpal ldan ye śes refers to Tāranātha. as the disciple of the Indian monk Buddhagupta (pp. 29, 49): Tāranātha himself also begins his *Bkaḥ babs bdus Idam* by invoking with great reverence his great *guru* (Edelsteinmine, p. I. *cf.* p. 116) of whom mention is also to be found in another work of Tāranātha, viz., the *Gsaṅ baḥi rnam t'ar* in which the dream is narrated that pre-told his imminent meeting with Buddhagupta. *Ibid.*, p. 686.

(16th century) India had not yet forgotten those great links of cultural relations which Buddhism had established between her and far away countries from Africa to Java". But its greatest importance lies in his account of the position of Buddhism in the various places and countries covered by the author's wide travels[1].

Buddhagupta's travels brought him to Karṇāṭaka.

"Then he started again east; so through Jārikhaṇḍa and Jagannātha[2] he went to Khaṣarpaṇa in Buntavarta[3] where he spent in prayer about twenty days. . . . Then he went to Tipurā[4] and to the high land of Tipurā where there is Kāśāraṇya or Devilkoṭā. For some days he remained in the temple erected by the Mahāsiddha Kṛṣṇācārya. Thence he proceeded to Ra k'an[5], and to its (other ?) places, Haribhañja[6]. Bu k'an[7] und Balgu[8]. *In all these countries there is a great community of monks, and the Buddhist teaching is widely spread.* He stopped therefore

1. For a detailed resumé of the text, see, Tucci, *op. cit.* But as we are here concerned with Burma, we at once go to the relevant point leaving the reader to gather the very interesting information furnished by the text from Dr. Tucci's admirable paper.
2. Jhāḍakhaṇḍa and Purī respectively, in Orissa.
3. Perhaps a corruption of Pundravardhana.
4. Certainly Tripurā, modern Tipperah.
5. Of course Arakan, known also to Tāranātha. It is not mentioned whether the route followed was by sea or land, but the text seems to point out to a land route connecting Tripurā with Arakan. Tucci thinks that Ra k'an was the general designation for Burma. This could hardly have been the case; had it been so there would have been no necessity of mentioning Bu k'an (= Pukam = Pagan) as a place separate from Ra k'an. He translates the relevant passage as "Ra k'an and to its places Haribhañja, etc.". Either the translation should be "Ra k'an and to other places (viz.), Haribhañja, Bu k'an and Balgu", or the text itself must be wrong. Ra k'an was never so powerful as to include Bu k'an.
6. Dr. Tucci suggests that this is a corruption of Haripuñjaya, north of Menam near Lamphun. Compare also Haripuñja in the *Sāsanavaṁsa;* the two seem to me to be identical. Further, can Haribhañja. - Haripuñjaya - Haripuñja be the same as Tāranātha's Muñjan? Tāranātha's group of places named in this connection is almost the same as Buddhagupata's, except Muñjan and Haribhañja.
7. Pukari = Pugāmā = Pagan.
8. Dr. Tucci identifies Balgu with Pegu. I consider it doubtful, for Tāranātha mentions Balgu and Pajigu (= Pegu) as two different countries; so does Buddhagupta. In the passage quoted here Paigu (= Pegu) is mentioned as a place distinct from Balgu. I cannot, however, offer any identification at present.

a long time and heard many treatises of the *sūtra* class *and as far as possible the law of the secret mantras* from paṇḍita Dharmākṣaghoṣa of the big *stūpas* in the temple of Haribhañja and equally from the lay paṇḍita Parhetanandaghoṣa in the country of Balgu. These *gurus* were the followers of Mahāsiddha Śāntipāda. Then he embarked again and went to the island of Dhanaśrī[1]. In this island also there are very many monks. There is a great stūpa of immense proportion which is called Śrīmad Dhānyakaṭaka, or the stūpa with the offering of *astukakāya*.... It takes about one day for its *pradakṣiṇa*. On the east there is a very big town where there is an enormous assemblage of merchants coming from different countries such as Cīna, P'ren gi (= Phiraṅga = mod. : Firingi) land and India. When he visited the Pratibimba Stūpa he saw the *maṇḍala* of the five *kulas* with Vairocana as their central essence, in the Jñānakāya stūpa the *maṇḍala* of the five *kulas* with Amitābha as the central essence, and in Śrīmad Dhānyakaṭaka with the *Maṇḍala* of the five *kulas* with Akṣobhya as the central essence. Then together with some merchants he visited some very small islands, such as another island in the middle of the sea called Potala, the island Paigu (= Pegu) and island occupied by the P'nen gi (probably, Portuguese) in which many medicinal herbs such as *jati and lesi* are produced, Sandhādvīpa, the great Suvarṇadvīpa, the great Suvarṇadvīpa (Sumatra), the small Suvarṇadvipa, Sūryadvipa, Candradvipa, Sarvadvīpa"[2].

Buddhagupta's evidence throws a different light on the Buddhism of Pagan. Here, as well as in Haribhañja and Balgu, there was a great community of monks, and the Buddhist teaching was widely spread. We cannot identify Haribhañja and Balgu, but they must be located somewhere in Lower Burma. We are sure of Pagan where in the sixteenth century the Theravāda was the most popular form of religion, widely practised by the people. Buddhagupta's evidence

1. i.e., Tennasserim, as I have suggested.
2. Tucci, *op. cit.*, pp. 697-698. Candradvīpa of this passage cannot, I think, be identified with the place of the same name in the Bakarganj district of Bengal, not far from the sea. It seems to be a generic name like Suvarṇadvīpa and Tāmradvīpa, and was applied to more than one island in the Bay of Bengal. The Small Suvarṇadvīpa may refer to one of the smaller islands near Sumatra. As for Sandhādvīpa, Sarvadvīpa and Sūryadvipa, I cannot at present offer any identification.

   Nor can I be sure of "the island in the middle of the sea called Potala". Buddhagupta's account seems to suggest that it was a Buddhist centre. Is it the same as Potalaka referred to in a Tumber of miniature epigraphs in the Cambridge MS. no. Add. 1643, and in the Asiatic Society of Bengal MS. no. A. 15? Compare nos. 16, 73 and 74 at the former and nos. 18 and 25 of the latter, in Foucher, *Iconographie Bouddhique*, pp. 192, 203, 210, 212.

seems to suggest that the Mahāyāna had by this time lost its influence in Pagan, but not in Haribhañja and Balgu where he heard *'as far as possible the law of the secret mantras'*. The implication of course is that in these countries the Mantrayāna was already on the wane.

In Tennasserim, however, the Mahāyāna seems to have been rather popular. Śrī Dhānyakaṭaka has been identified with Amarāvatī on the Kistna, though, according to certain Tibetan texts there is a place of the name also in Tibet. In any case, the *stūpa,* Śrīmad Dhānyakaṭaka referred to by Buddhagupta must be sought for somewhere in Tennasserim, though it is permissible to conjecture that it may have been erected by Mahāyānist emigrants from Śrī Dhānyakaṭaka in Southern India. It is however strange that no such *stūpa* or it remains exist, so far as I know, in Tennasserim. The Cambridge MS. no. Add. 1643 has one miniature representing a *stūpa* and inscribed: *Ambuviṣaye Śrī-Śrī -Dhānya-caityaḥ*[1] which locates a Dhānya Caitya, evidently a *stūpa,* in the Ambuviṣaya, which, I infer, may have been situated on a sea-coast.

It is curious that native tradition and chronicles preserve no memory of this aspect of Buddhism which must have existed side by side with the Hīnayāna, even after the great Theravāda reformation of Anawrahta in the elventh and of Dhammaceti in the fifteenth century. The latter thus seems to have denied the existence of the Mahāyāna and its allied cults by ignoring therm altogether.

1. Fol. 218, V°, 2, p. 62; Foucher, *Iconographie Bouddhique,* p. 202. Foucher describes the miniature as follows: "Stūpa blanc, assez simple, surmonté d'un lourd parasol. Balustrade quatre portes par trois desquelles entrent des personnages (deux bleus et un rouge)". It is interesting to compare this with what Buddhagupta says about the *pradakṣiṇa* of the Śrīmad Dhānyakaṭaka Caitya.

6
When and Whence Did Sanskrit Buddhism Penetrate Burma?

Evidence of Epigraphic Records

We have now to face the last stage of our enquiry: when and whence did Sanskrit Buddhism, the Mahāyāna with its allied cults, in particular, come to be introduced in Burma.

We have seen that a considerable number of Sanskrit inscriptions on stone and terracotta votive tablets have been brought to light from the ruins of Hmawza and Pagan. It is significant that the script of these records are either Gupta-Brāhmī of about the seventh century or Eastern Nāgarī of the ninth, tenth and succeeding centuries, both current in those countries of Eastern India now roughly covered by the modern provinces of Bihar and Bengal. It is evident therefore that these regions were the original home of these records. In Hmawza, Sanskrit already makes its appearance about the seventh century, closely following on the Pāli records discovered there which, however, are written in a script current in the Andhra-Pallava region of South India in about the fifth and sixth centuries. These Pāli records obviously owe their inspiration to Theravāda Buddhism, Sanskrit may have been the language of either or of both Northern Buddhism and Brahmanism which was well-known in the ancient Pyu capital and was practised by at least a certain section of the people. But not a single Sanskrit record, so far recovered from the ruins of ancient Prome, can be attributed to Brahmanism; in fact, all of them belong to Buddhism, and can be attributed either to the Mūlasarvāstivādīns, a Hīnayānist sect using Sanskrit as their sacred language, or to those Northern Buddhists who were known as followers of the Mahāyāna. The earlier wave of Sanskrit Buddhism in Burma seems, however, to be that of the Mūlasarvāstivādīns, as I have tried to show; this made itself felt in ancient Prome sometime about the seventh century.

About the ninth and tenth centuries, the Mahāyāna gained the upper hand in Eastern India, and throughout the monastic establishments in Bihar and Bengal, gods and goddesses of the Northern pantheon, held sway. This seems to have brought in a corresponding change in the relative position of the Sarvāstivāda and the Mahāyāna in Burma as well. The Sanskrit used in the short epigraphs on terracotta votive tablets of the ninth, tenth, eleventh and the succeeding centuries is no longer the language of the Sarvāstivādīns; it is the language of those Mahāyānists who constantly poured into Burma and brought with them small votive tablets, representing sacred shrines or images and inscribed with the Buddhist formula. The small terracotta tablet recovered from the ruins of Hmawza and representing a standing image of Tārā around which is inscribed the Buddhist formula, is one of the numerous tablets that were taken by pilgrims to the capital cities of Burma. The later wave of the Buddhists in Burma seems therefore to have been initiated by the Mahāyānists; this began to make itself felt, so far as we can ascertain from archaeological evidence, from about the ninth or tenth century from which time Mahāyāna gods and goddesses begin to make their appearance. It is significant that not a single image, definitely identifiable as a Mahāyānist divinity, may on stylistic grounds be said to antedate this period[1], though Sanskrit seems to have been known in Pagan earlier for at least a century, and in Prome already for about two or three centuries. But whether one agrees or not with the relative chronological position of the Sarvāstivāda and the Mahāyāna in Burma, the evidence of the epigraphic records points unmistakably to the fact (a) that Sanskrit Buddhism was introduced in Burma not later than the seventh century (b) that, as indicated by the abundant and continuous supply of terracorta votive tablets with legends in Sanskrit, written in Nāgari characters, and represenring Mahāyāna divinities, this Sanskrit Buddhism, the Mahāyāna with its allied cults, in particular,

1. It is true that there have been unearthed from the ruins of ancient Prome a few reliefs on stone and terracotta tablets representing the Buddha flanked by the Bodhisattvas, Maitreya and Avalokiteśvara, that may stylistically be dated before the ninth century; but it is well-known that in Burma, these two Bodhisattvas were never considered to belong exclusively to the Mahāyāna pantheon.

seems to have received a new lease of life from about the ninth and tenth centuries and continued its career, in and around Pagan, till about the end of the fourteenth century, and (c) that the original home of this Sanskrit Buddhism of Burma was the North-Eastern provinces of India.

Evidence of Sculptures, Bronzes and Paintings

Hmawza

Let us now consider how these conclusions are in a general way corroborated by a stylistic consideration of the sculptures, bronzes and paintings representing Mahāyāna divinities, and by instances of intimate historical inter-relations between Eastern India and Burma.

At the very outset one must leave out of consideration the beautiful bronze image of Avalokiteśvara from Hmawza which has been described in a previous chapter[1]. The facial type, the broad and hardened forehead, the deep eyes and the bow-like moustache are all strongly reminiscent of old Cambodian tradition, and it is not unlikely that the image was somehow carried over from its original home to the city of the Pyus.

First of all we have to consider the two headless Buddha images with Sanskrit inscriptions recovered from the ruins of Hmawza, the one from Kan-wet-khaung-kon, and the other from a mound at Pyogingyi-kon[2]. It has already been pointed out that stylistically both the images belong definitely to the late Gupta tradition of Eastern India of about the sixth and seventh centuries. The ruins of Hmawza have yielded a number of stone sculptures and terra-cotta reliefs mostly representing Buddhist subjects and belonging to this same art tradition familiar in the Magadhan region during the 6th-8th centuries. The same observation would hold good also with regard to the stone reliefs recovered from Hmawza representing Avalokiteśvara and Maitreya flanking the Buddha. In connection with a similar relief found at the ruins of the Zegu Pagoda (Hmawza) Sir John Marshall states that the sculpture derives its style from

1. *An. R.A.S.I.*, 1911-12, pl. LXVIII, fig. 6.
2. *Ibid.*, 1927-28, pp. 127-28 and plate; *ibid.*, 1928-29, p. 108, pl. LI, b.

the familiar Gupta tradition of Eastern India of about the seventh and eighth centuries[1].

But the two small images of Bodhisattvas, one in bronze and another in gold, recovered from the ruins at Yindaik-kwin, Hmawza[2], seem to belong to an entirely different art-tradition, and executed at a later date. Artistically, they appear to affiliate themselves to the art of the Pālas of Bihar and Bengal. A stylistic consideration of the few unidentified images of Bodhisattvas represented on terracotta tablets bearing Sanskrit Nāgari inscriptions also leads to the same conclusion. All of them, including the image of Jambhala and the large-sized unidentified Bodhisattva figure from the same locality, belong to what is called the Eastern School of art and can be dated on stylistic grounds from about the ninth to about the eleventh century.

Pagan

I have elsewhere attempted an artistic examination of the sculptures and bronzes of Pagan[3]. It will suffice to repeat here the conclusions arrived at, and bring out their significance in connection with our present subject. The majority of the Mahāyānist images of Pagan belong, on the ground of style, to about the eleventh and twelfth centuries, and the wall-paintings to as late as the thirteenth (*cf.* the paintings of the Nandamañña temple, built in 1248). It follows, therefore, so far as can be judged from images and paintings extant, that the Mahāyāna with its allied cults remained an active force in Pagan, at least with a considerable section of her people, even after the Theravāda had become the state religion after the conquest of Thaton in 1057, and it was during the suzerainty of the Anawrahta dynasty (1044-1283) - those two centuries and a quarter of glorious and magnificent mediaeval kingship - that the Mahāyāna and other cults of Northern Buddhism had their palmy days side by side with the much more popular Theravāda.

In nearly all the images, particularly in the bronze images of Lokanātha seated in *lalitāsans* from the Ānanda Museum, Pagan, in the stone image of Mañjuśrī from the same shelter, in the image

1. *An. R.A.S.B.*, 1909- 10, Art. 33.
2. *An. R.A.S.I.*, 1928-29, p. 105, pl. LII, a, c.
3. Ray, "Sculptures and bronzes from Pagan", *J.I.S.O.A.*, July, 1934.

which I have identified as Vajrasattva in *yab-yum*, in the stone reliefs representing Avalokiteśvara and Maitreya flanking the Buddha, in the image of Tārā from the Myothit town, there can easily be noticed a distinct physiognomical type and a particular method of treatment which, though slightly varying from one to the other, may at once be said to be connected with the well-known and contemporary art tradition of Eastern India that flourished during the centuries covered by the rule of the Pālas and Senas of Bengal and Bihar. Even the dress and ornaments and poses and attitudes have a very close affinity with those of the numerous examples in stone and bronze of the Eastern School[1].

Still more convincing is the evidence of the wall-paintings which, from a stylistic point of view, can be classed roughly into two groups: one well-represented group plainly derives its style from those of contemporary miniature paintings of Bengal; the other group shows a very close affinity with contemporary Nepalese paintings and Jain paintings of Western India, both of which in their turn are closely related with the Bengal MSS. paintings[2]. This is indicated by a comparative study of the wall-paintings of the Kubaukkyi, the Abeyadana, the Thanbula and similar temples, on the one hand, and those of the Paya-thon-zu and Nandamañña temples on the other. A comparison of these two parallel traditions in Burma with the miniatures of the *Aṣtasahasra-prajñāpāramita* MSS, in the Cambridge University Library (Add. 1643) and in the library of the Asiatic Society of Bengal (A. 15) and contemporary Nepalese paintings reveals that they are very much alike in features and physiognomy of the personages they depict, in their poses and attitudes, dress and ornaments, and above all in their flat modelling of the contours of their body and in the clean Sweep of their lines. The conclusion is almost irresistible that the art-tradition of these wall-paintings of Pagan was imported from contemporary Bengal and Nepal. Here in these countries was fostered, it is well-known, a school of painting that continued

1. *Cf.* Kramrisch, "Pāla and Sena Sculptures", *Rūpam*, Calcutta.
2. As all these are well-known to scholars, it is not necessary to go into details. Reference may be made to *Rūpam*, 1922, no. 2, Vredenberg, "Continuity of pictorial tradition in India"; *J.I.S.O.A.*, 1934, I. ii, Kramrisch, "Nepalese Paintings".

the pictorial tradition of the classical period during the 10th-13th centuries.

During this long period, Eastern India, comprising the countries of modern Bengal, Bihar and Nepal, was the stronghold of Mahāyāna Buddhism and its allied cults partly saturated with Tantrism. While Nālandā was one of the best known centres in Bihar, no less important were Samataṭa, Harikela and other localities in Bengal where particularly the cults of Lokanātha and Tārā, thrived (*cf.* the miniatures of the Cambridge and Asiatic Society MSS.). The Theravāda was at a discount, and even Sarvāstivāda which in I-tsing's time was so widely prevalent, seems to have lost its influence.

The evidence of cultural relations between Burma and Eastern India during these centuries is almost overwhelming. The large number of terracotta votive tablets evidently carried over from Eastern India to Pagan and other localities, the Mahā-bodhi temple of Pagan, an unsuccessful imitation of the Bodh-gayā temple, the repeated missions of Pagan kings to the shrine at Bodh-gayā, and the accounts, contained in Burmese chronicles, of Burmese merchants visiting the ports of Bengal, all bear testimony to the intimate relations that existed between Burma and Eastern India. One piece of evidence the importance of which for the present subject has not yet been fully realised, may be detailed here. It is furnished by two accounts of the reigns of Kyanzittha, Alaungsithu and Narathu recorded in Burmese chronicles. These romantic accounts are well-known in Burma and are acted on the stage to this day[1]. Here it will suffice to say that while one refers to the celebrated love-romance of the Prince of Pateikkara with the only daughter of Kyanzittha, the other refers to the marriage of a Pateikkara princess by Narathu, the eventual murder of the princess by Narathu, and the consequent counter-murder of Narathu by the desperados sent by the king of Pateikkara in revenge. The identification of Pateikkara was for years a puzzle to scholars in Burma, though the identity of the kingdom with Paṭikārā in the Tipperah district (included in ancient Harikel) had been established

1. Reference may be made to Phayre, *History of Burma,* pp. 37, 40; Harvey, *History of Burma; An. R.A.S.B.,* 1923, p. 32,

long ago[1]. This identification is also supported by the position of the kingdom according to the Burmese chronicles, and now finally established by the Maynāmatī Copper-plate of Raṇavaṅkamalla Harikāladeva[2]. It proves once more that for about a century (1084-1190) Pagan maintained a very intimate relation with Pateikkara or Paṭṭikera in ancient Harikela which was reputed as a centre of Māhayāna Buddhism. The Maynāmatī Copper-plate seems also to indicate that Paṭikārā (the Indian form of Burmese Pateikkara) was a centre of worship of the Mahāyāna goddess Durgottārā as well as a seat of the *Sahaja* cult, besides having been well-known for the worship of another Mahāyāna god, Lokanātha.

We have been able to adduce numerous indications regarding the time when and the locality whence the Mahāyāna and its allied cults were introduced in Burma. This happened not later than the ninth or tenth century, possibly even earlier; it flourished in Pagan during the eleventh, twelfth and thirteenth centuries after which period Pagan sank into singificance. Strange to say the period coincides almost exactly with the time when the Theravāda was enjoying a new lease of life under the patronage of the kings of the Pagan dynasty. The Mahāyāna and its allied cults were in all probability, as we have seen above, introduced in Burma from the region that now comprises Bihar and Bengal. This, again, is curious and interesting; for throughout these centuries, Pagan always kept her face turned towards Ceylon for guidance and inspiration in all matters relating to the newly introduced faith of the Theravāda. The metropolis sent her masters of the religion, Uttarajīva and Capata and a host of others in succession, to Ceylon to equip themselves for the great work of reformation in Burma through the purer faith of the Theravāda. It is significant that these *theras* did not go to Kāñcīpuram or Kāverīpattanam whence Burma must originally have received the Southern form of Buddhism. Evidently, these and other places in the eastern coastal regions of South India had lost their importance as centres of Buddhist learning, and Ceylon had superseded them. This is confirmed by the Kalyāṇī inscriptions of king Dhammaceti which prove that Ceylon had by the later half

1. *Tripurā Rājamālā*, pp. 4-6.
2. *Ind. Hist. Quart.*, IX, i, pp. 282-89.

of the eleventh century grown to so great importance as a Buddhist centre that *mahātheras* from such diverse and distant countries as Tamralipti, Kamboja and Kāñcīpuram flocked to that island to receive training and inspiration.

It is now easier for us to see how our conclusions as to the introduction and spread of the Mahāyāna and its allied cults agree in the main with the account of the spread of Buddhism as outlined by Tāranātha and supplemented by the testimonies of Buddhagupta and the *Pag Sam Jon Zang*. The sum-total of what Taranātha says in this connection is that it was during the rule of the Pālas, but more particularly, during that of the (four) Senas of Bengal that the Mahāyāna made itself strongly felt in Pagan, Pegu and Arakan, so much so that even the monks of Madhyadeśa received their training in these and other centres of the Koki land, and that it was from Bihar and Bengal that the religion was introduced there. This agrees remarkably well with the conclusions we have arrived at from a study of the archaeological remains.

Conclusions

The domain of Sanskrit Buddhism in Burma may, for the sake of convenience, be divided in two divisions: (a) Lower Burma, with its political centre at the Pyu capital of Prome and later on at the Talaing capital of Thaton; (b) Upper Burma with its centre at Pagan. The earliest form of Sanskrit Buddhism is probably the Mūlasarvāstivāda-nikāya which appears to have been introduced in the old Pyu capital from Magadha in Eastern India sometime before the seventh century. This is suggested by the discovery of a number of Buddhist images exhibiting the later Gupta style and, some of them, inscribed with Sanskrit inscriptions in the Gupta-Brāhmī script of Eastern India, and by the evidence of I-tsing as well. The Mūlasarvāstivāda-nikāya seems thus to have flourished side by side with the Sthaviravāda-nikāya which had been introduced there, evidently from the coast of Coromandel and the Telegu country, some time before the sixth century. It was undoubtedly the religion much more widely professed than either the Sarvāstivāda or Brahmanism. This seems to have been the state of religion in ancient Prome till at least as late as the eighth and ninth centuries when Mahāyāna Buddhism seems to have made its appearance to add another factor to the already varied religious life of the capital. Gods and goddesses of the Mahāyāna pantheon must have been worshipped there till as late as the tenth century; this is determined not only by the palaeography of the inscriptions on the numerous terracotta votive tablets found there, but also by the style of the few images of the Mahāyāna pantheon recovered from the ruins of the old city. They further tend to prove that the Mahāyāna in Lower Burma was introduced from Eastern India, more definitely from the Magadhan region, the intercourse having been maintained by sea which was probably the easiest route to reach the ports of peninsular Burma.

But already by about the ninth century, if not earlier, ancient Prome was losing its political importance; in the race for power and supremacy the Talaings were outwitting the exhausted Pyus. The Talaings seem to have had their centre at Thaton, then just on the sea-shore, where an active centre of Theravāda Buddhism was gradually growing up. By about the middle of the eleventh century when Manuha was on the throne of Thaton, the city swarmed with learned monks in a hundred monasteries whose libraries contained all the wisdom of the faith recorded in Pali[1]. The Mahāyāna seems scarcely to have penetrated there; we have at least no evidence to that effect.

We learn a different story in respect to Pagan and other centres of Upper Burma. If Tāranātha deserves any credit, the introduction of Mahāyāna Buddhism in Burma lies as far back as at least the fifth century, for, according to him, the Mahāyāna was first introduced in the Koki land by the pupils of Vasubandhu 'from which time it continued to exist uninterruptedly'. This finds an indirect confirmation in the statement of the Burmese chronicles, e.g., of the *Hmannan,* to the effect that the 'religion (Buddhism) gradually grew weak from the reign of king Thaittang (c. 516-523), founder of the city of Tampavati (= Thamahti, near Pagan), and because there was no *Piṭaka* or sacred writ, only the doctrines of the Ari lords at Thamahti were generally adopted'[2]. This seems to suggest that the cult of Ari, originally a Mahāyāna cult, was already known there before the beginning of the sixth century. But the most flouri-shing period of the Mahāyāna and allied cults in Pagan and other centres of Upper Burma must have begun from the ninth century (from the reign of the Pāla king Dharmapāla, according to Tāranātha), and lasted until at least the end of the thirteenth. This

1. Compare the accounts of the invasion and eventual conquest of Thaton by Anawrahta, 1057, in the *Hmannan,* the *Sāsanavaṁsa,* the Kalyāṇī inscriptions, and other Burmese chronicles. The cumulated evidence seems to convey the impression of a very flourishing existence of the Theravāda in the Talaing capital in the middle of the eleventh century.
2. According to the Burmese chronicles, Buddhism came to be introduced in Burma even during the life time of the Buddha himself, and that it retained its purity till the cult of the Ari (originally a Mahāyāna cult) was introduced wheri the purer religion began to decline (in the opinion of later Theravādī chroniclers).

is testified to not only by Tāranātha and the author of the *Pag Sam Jon Zang,* but also by extant images of deities of the Mahāyāna and Tantrayāna, and by the no less important evidence furnished by a large number of Sanskrit inscriptions on terracotta votive tablets. As to the country from where these cults were introduced in Burma, all available evidence points to Bihar and Bengal, more particularly to Bengal, at least in respect of the later phases of the cults when they came to be saturated with Tantric rites. The prevalence of Tantrayāna is proved by the cult of the Aris, but more definitely by the wall-paintings of the Paya-thon-zu and the Nandamañña Termples and one or two images in stone and bronze. According to Tāranātha, the Mantrayāna and Kālacakrayāna were also known in Pagan; the introduction of the latter is proved by the existence of Kālacakra texts in the monastic libraries of Upper Burma as late as the middle of the fifteenth century. All these evidently were introduced from Bengal, and perhaps also from Bihar, the intercourse between the two countries being maintained probably both by land and sea. A land route through Assam and Manipur was still known in the seventeenth and eighteenth centuries.

According to Taranātha, Mahāyāna Buddhism and its allied cults existed in Pegu and Arakan as well, and the account of Buddhagupta's travels seems to indicate that it was known also in Tennasserim. But, unfortunately we have no evidence from independent sources to verify their testimony, though there is nothing antecedently improbable in it.

It has already been pointed out that the floursishing period of the Mahāyāna and its allied cults coincides for the greater part with the golden period of the great Theravāda reformation (c. 1057–c. 1300 A.D.). In fact, the Theravāda became the religion of the state and the people who gradually gave up their allegiance to older faiths; Mahāyāna Buddhism could hardly keep pace with the growing popularity of the new religion in which the people found a simpler and purer faith, and soon it became a lost cause, though it still continued to attract a minor section of the people. The attitude of the Theravāda towards the Mahāyāna and its allied cults, except with the degenerated sect of the Aris, seems to have been one of absolute tolerance. This is suggested by the existence of Mahāyānist and Tantric places of worship not very far from the heart of the capital city, as well as by the finds of Mahāyāna images in what were presumably places of worship of the Theravādīns, and, as already stated, also by the Nandamañña inscription of 1248. Even with regard to the Aris, the attitude of the court and people does not seem to have been very cruel and severe. Anawrahta's drive against them must have been only partially successful; the very fact that they had a strong centre with temples and monasteries just on the outskirts of the metropolis proves that they continued to maintain themselves and were tolerated by the people around. There is also evidence to show that their daily necessities of monastic life were attended to by the court and perhaps also by lay men.

Mahāyāna Buddhism and its allied cults in Pagan, when we see them in existence, were after all practised by only a section of the people who, we may infer, had a full-fledged organisation of their Own, but the Theravāda being the much more popular and powerful religion could well afford to look at its vanquished rival with a confident smile. The two faiths seem to have lived side by side till at last the Theravāda, always with the support of the throne, was able to emerge completely triumphant and wipe out even the memory of its rival. But in the course of centuries of close neighbourhood, the Theravāda of Burma came to absorb some of the elements of its sister faith, and some of the gods of the Mahāyāna pantheon, e.g., Avalokiteśvara and Maitreya, were even adopted by the Theravādīns. This is perhaps why Tāranātha says that in the Koki countries the "Mahāyāna and the Hīnayāna were not always distinguishable".

Bibliography

(This bibliography is not claimed to be exhaustive; publications which have been used mainly as references are excluded, as they have been mentioned in their proper places in the text and footnotes. It includes only those publications that have direct bearing on the subject of this monograph, touching on it in more or less details).

Archaeological Survey of Burma, *Annual Reports of the Archaeological Survey, Burma Circle,* 1901-26. Superintendent, Government Printing, Rangoon.

——Annual Album of photographs of sculptures, bronzes, paintings, monuments, inscriptions, etc., of Burma, Office of the Archaeological Survey, Burma Circle, Mandalay.

Archaeological Survey of India, *Annual Reports of the Archaeological Survey of India,* 1901-to date, Simla and Delhi.

Bode, Mabel, *The Pālī Literature of Burma,* Royal Asiatic Society, London.

——*Sāsanavaṁsa,* Pāli Text Society, London.

Burma Research Society, *Journal of the Burma Research Society,* 1910-to date, Rangoon.

Duroiselle, Charles, "The Aris of Burma and Tantric Buddhism", in *An. R.A.S.I.,* 1915-16, pp. 79-93.

——[Stray notes, mainly in the *An, R.A.S.B., An. R.A.S.I., J.B.R.S.,* and the *B.E.F.E.O*.].

Finot, Louis, "Un nouveau document sur le buddhisme birman", in *J.A., XX,* Joul-Aout, 1912, p. 121 ff.

Forchammer, E., *The Jardine Prize: an essay on the sources and development of Burmese Law,* Rangoon.

Government of Burma, *Inscriptions of Pagan, Pinya and Ava.* Superintendent, Government Printing, Rangoon, 1892.

——*Inscriptions copied from the stones collected by Bodawpaya,* 2 vols. Superintendent, Government Printing, Rangoon, 1897.

——*Inscriptions collected in Upper Burma,* 2 vols. Superintendent, Government Printing, Rangoon, 1900 and 1903.

——*Original Inscriptions collected by king Bodawpaya in Upper Burma now in the Patodawgyi Pagoda, Amarapura,* Superintendent, Government Printing, Rangoon, 1913.

Harvey, G.E., *History of Burma,* Oxford University Press, 1925.

Hmannan Yazawin, 3 vols. Upper Burma Press, Mandalay.

I-tsing, *I-tsing's records of the Western World,* edited and translated by J. Takakusu, Clarendon Press. Oxford.

Luce, G. H., "Burma, with special reference to her relations with China", in *J.B.R.S,* XIV, ii, August, 1925.

Maung Tin, Pe and Luce, G. H., *The Glass Palace Chronicle.* Oxford University Press.

Ray, Niharranjan, "Lokanātha and other Mahāyāna. Gods in Burma", in *Buddhistic Studies,* Vol. I, Calcutta, 1931.

——"Mahāyānist and Tantric Texts in Burma", in *Indian Culture,* Vol. I, no. 2, pp. 282-84.

Sumpa Khan-po Yeśepal Joz, *Pag Sam Jon Zang, I,* edited by Sarat Chandra Das, Presidency Jail Press, Calcutta, 1908, pp. 123-24.

Tāranātha, *Tāranātha's Geschichte des Buddhismus in Indien,* translated from Tibetan by Schiefner, St. Petersburg, 1869.

Tin, U, "Mahāyānism in Pagan", in *J.B.R.S.;* XIX, ii, August, 1929. pp. 36-42.

Taw Sein Ko, *Burmese Sketches,* Rangoon.

Tucci, G., "The sea and land travels of a Buddhist Sādhu in the sixteenth century", in *Ind. Hist. Quart.,* VII, no. 4, December, 1931, pp. 683-702.

Watters, *Yuan Chwang,* 2 vols. London.

Index

A

Abeyadana 56ff, 92
Abhayagiri 79
Abhayakara 76, 78, 81
Abhidharma 74,78, 81
Acawkwama 42
Ādityavarman 13
Africa 84, 85
Akṣobhya 13, 86
Alaungsithu 42, 93
Amarāvatī 4, 87
Amarendrapura 11
Ambuviṣaya 87
Amitābha 46, 86
Amogasiddhi 46
Ānandacandra 78
Ānanda Museum 41, 46, 47, 51, 91
Ānanda Temple 2, 45, 48
Anawrahta (Anaorata) 2, 14, 30, 31, 33, 42, 57, 64ff, 83, 87, 91, 97
Anawrahtaminsaw 64, 65
Andhra 4, 88
Angkor Thom 11, 12
Aṅguttara Nikāya 4
Aniruddha (Anuruddha) 42, 68
Annam 24, 26
Antarvedī 76
Aparāntaka 73, 77
Arakan 43, 77ff., 85, 98
Archipelago 84
Arhanta 68
Ari 16, 17, 62ff., 97ff
Ari-gyi-do-ahnwe 66
Arimaddanapura 64
Arpacana 46
Aruṇa 60
Ārya 63
Asam 74
A-shan 29
Asia I, 40, 92
Asoka (Aśoka) 3, 77, 80
Assam 14, 15, 74, 77, 80, 98
Aṣṭasahasra-prajñāpāramitā 92
Atiśa 10
Ava 34, 66, 67, 68, 79
Avalokiteśvara 11, 40ff, 89, 90, 92, 99
Ayuthia 8, 23

B

Bagchi 11, 37
Bakarganj 86
Bālaputradeva 10
Balgu 77, 80, 85, 87
Bali 2, 28
Bandyaghaṭi 73
Baṅgāla 74
Baṅgāladeśa 74
Banteai Chmar 11
Barabuḍur 9, 10, 14, 58
Baros 28

Bātī 6
Bhattacharya 46, 47, 51, 61
Bawbawgyi Pagoda 3
Bayon 11
Beal 24
Benares 45
Bengal 10, 13, 14, 31, 33, 37, 49, 58, 70, 73, 74, 76, 79, 80, 82, 86, 88, 89, 91, 92, 93, 94, 95, 98
Bengali 16, 31, 32, 34
Bergaigne 7
Bernard Free Library 43
Bhangala 74, 76, 77
Bhaṭaghaṭi 73
Bhattasali 49
Bhojanagara 29
Bihar 14, 13, 33, 76, 80, 82, 88, 89, 91, 92, 93, 94, 95, 98
Bidagataik 2
Bilhana 75
Blagden 19
Blobzan-dpal-ldan-yeśes 84
Bodawpaya 79
Bode 34, 35, 69.
Bodh-gayā 21, 33, 75, 93
Borneo 6, 7, 28, 30
Brahmā 13, 43
Brahmanism 5, 7, 8
Brāhmī 19, 20, 22, 30, 88, 96
Buddhaghosa (ghoṣa) 3, 4
Buddhagupta 6, 72, 84ff., 95
Buddhamitra 76
Buddhapurāṇa 73
Buddhasena 77
Bühler 4
Bu k'an 85
Bukit Muriam 6
Buntavarta 85
Burney 68

C

Cālukya 75
Cambay 36
Campa 8, 12, 14, 23, 27, 29, 77, 80, 84
Campitala (Campita) 49
Candra 76
Candradvīpa 86
Candrakaragupta 76, 81
Candraprabhā 46
Canton 27
Capata 5, 94
Cauk-hpaya-hla 50
Ceram 29
Ceylon 1, 5, 8, 29, 30, 78, 79, 94
Chakravarti 9
Chatterji 7, 9, 10, 11, 12, 13
Chhabra 6, 9
Ch'ang Chun 25
Chau-ju-cua 25, 26, 78
Chavannes 23ff., 27, 78
Chen-la 27
Chia-mo-lang-chia 23, 24, 27
Chih-ngan 27
Ch'in-t'u 25
China 24, 27, 29
Chindwin 15
Cīna 86
Coedés 7, 9, 25, 26, 78
Cola (Coḍa) 5
Cordier 25, 76
Coromandel 96

D

Das 10
Daśabala 76
Devapāla 10
Devīkoṭa 85
Dhammaceti 2, 67, 87, 94

Dhammadassi 64, 65
Dhanaśrī 79, 86
Dhanaśrīdvīpa 78, 79
Dhānya Caitya 87
Dhānya Kaṭaka 86, 87
Dharmadása 75
Dharmakīrti 36, 37
Dharmākṣaghoṣa 86
Dharmapāla 36, 78, 97
Dharmaśāstras 12
Dharmottara 36
Dikshit 19
Dīpaṅkara 10, 45
Divine-Land 29
Dong-Duong 12
*D*pal-*b*rtsegsrakṣita 37
Durgottārā 94
Duroiselle 17, 19, 32, 33, 47, 53, 62, 63, 67, 68, 69, 70
Dvāravatī 8, 23, 24, 26

E

Eliot 13
Er-laṅga 28

F

Fa-hien 8
Fan-chih 79
Ferrand 15, 25, 26, 28, 29
Finot 3, 4, 62, 63, 70, 81, 83
Firingi 86
Forchammer 34, 35
Fo-shih-pu-lo 29
Foucher 12, 49, 86, 87
Foulkes 3
Fou-nan (Fü-nan) 6, 7, 27
Further-India 1, 7, 12, 24, 27, 33

G

Gaṅgā 76
Gautama (Gotama) 42, 45
Ghazni 75
Girivarta 77
Glass palace Chronicle 15
Godāvarī 6
Gorakṣa 77
Goran 29
Grantha 6, 12
Great Black Mountain 23
Grub c'en Buddha-gupptbaḥi... 84
Gsaṅ-bahi ruam t'ar 84
Guhyadatta 74
Gulun 29
Guṇavarman 7
Gunong Jērai 26
Gupta 19, 20, 22, 30, 88, 96
Gurun 29

H

Hackmann 3
Halāhala 42
Haṁsāvati 80
Haribhañja 85, 86, 87
Hariharālaya 11
Harihariharivāhanod bhava Lokeśvara 42
Harikāladeva 94
Harikel (Harikela) 49, 93
Haripuñja 85
Haripuñjaya 85
Haritasena 77
Harivarmadeva 37
Harivikrama 19, 20
Harṣa Śilāditya 74
Harvey 62, 93
Hasam 74, 77
Hayagrīva 40, 47, 49, 50, 60
Hchi bslu-ba sgrol-ma dharmoḥi sgrub-thabs 38
Hchi bslubaḥi man-ṅag-gi sgrol-maḥi sgrub thabs 38

Hetubindu 36, 37
Hetubindu-ṭīkā 36
Hevajra 12
Hīnayāna 3, 7, 16, 22, 29, 30, 43, 77, 83, 87, 99
Hinduism 22
Hirth 25
Hiuen Thsang 21, 23, 24ff., 79
Hmannan (Yazawin) 2, 62, 63, 66, 68, 70, 97
Hmazwa 3, 4, 20, 23, 40, 41, 43, 47, 82, 83, 88, 89, 90
Ho-ling 27, 28, 78
Hüber 70

I

I-hsūan 27
Ikhtiyar-ud-din-Muhammad 75
I-lang 27
Ilaṅgāsogam 25, 26
India 1, 4, 5, 8, 12, 14, 15, 19, 20, 21, 23, 24, 28, 29, 30, 33, 34, 58, 76, 78, 83, 84, 86, 87, 88, 89, 90, 91, 92, 94, 96
Indian Archipelago 8
Indo-China 1, 5, 9
Indonesia 1, 5, 7, 9, 12, 33
Indra 43, 75
Indradatta 73
Indravarman 12
Irrawady 15
Islam 75
Iśvara 77

J

I-tsing 8, 9, 21ff., 33, 93, 96
Jagaddala 76
Jagannātha 85
Jaiya 78, 79
Jambhala 40, 47, 91
Jambi 28
Japan 37
Jardine 34, 35
Jārikhaṇḍa 85
Java 8, 9, 11, 12, 13, 14, 24, 26, 27, 28, 29, 30, 40, 58, 78, 85
Jayacandravarman 19, 20
Jayadeva 74
Jaya Indravarman 12
Jayasura 42
Jayavarman 7
Jayavarman II 11, 12
Jayavarman V 11
Jhāḍakhaṇḍa 85
Jinamitra 36
Jñānakaragupta 76
Jñānakāya 86
Johor 28.
Jonarāja 75

K

Kālacakra 37, 38, 39, 78, 83
Kālacakrayāna 98
Kadamba 4, 22, 30
Ka-lang-ka 21
Kalasan 9, 10
Kaliṅga 5, 21
Kalyāṇī 2, 67, 94, 97
Kāmalaṅka 23, 24, 25, 26, 27
Kamboja 7, 8, 11, 12, 14, 27, 40, 76, 77, 80, 81, 84, 95
Kāmarūpa 77
Kāmaśāstras 34
Kānāḍā-Telegu 4, 22, 30
Kāñcīpuram 4, 94, 95
Karṇāṭaka 85
Kāśāraṇya 85
Kāśasena 75
Kashmir 36, 73
Kaṭāha 10
Kāverī 6

Kāverīpattanam 4, 94.
Kan-wet-khaung-kon 19, 20, 22, 90
Kedah 6, 10, 26
Kĕlurak 9
Keśinī 46
Khaṣarpana 42, 85
Kinmungyon 47
Koki 38, 73, 77, 78, 80, 81, 82, 83, 84, 95, 97, 99
Kra 25
Kramrisch 92
Krĕtanagara 13
Krom 9, 12, 14, 29.
Kṛṣṇācārya 85
Kṣemendrabhadra 73
Kubaukkyi 49, 58, 92
Kukis 80
K'u-lun 29
Kuñjarakarṇa 13
Kyawza 69
Kyanzittha 57, 93
Kyundawza 4

L

Laghukālacakratantrarāja-ṭīkā 37, 38
Laghukālacakra-ṭīkā 37
Lamphun 85
Lang-chia 78
Lang-chia (-shu) 23ff
Lang-ya 23
Lang-ya-hsiu 26
Lang-ya-hsü 25, 26
Lang-ya-hsun 25
Lang-sakā 25
Laṅkāsu 23, 24
Lāṭa 28, 29, 75
Lavasena 75, 76
Lēnkasuka 25, 26
Levi 79
Liang-shu 25, 26
Ligor 9, 26
Ling-ya-ssu 25
Ling-yu-ssu-chia 25, 26
Lin-i 8, 23, 27, 29
Locac 25
Lokanātha 10, 16, 40ff., 93, 94
Lokeśvara 11, 12, 42
Luce 24, 25, 26, 29, 50, 58, 59, 64

M

Madamaliṅgam 78
Madhyadeśa 30, 78, 81, 95
Magadha 13, 20, 21, 28, 30, 33, 74, 75, 76, 78, 81, 90, 96
Magwe 45
Mahā-bodhi 93
Mahākālacakka 36, 37
Mahākālacakka-ṭīkā 36
Mahākālacakra 37, 38
Mahāmuni 43
Mahārāja Van Tawkri 43
Mahāsaṁghika-nikāya 28
Mahasin 28
Mahāvihāra 79
Mahāyānist sthavira 21
Mahmud 75
Meitreya 40ff., 89, 90, 92, 99
Majapahit 25
Makāras 13
Malay 9
Malay Archipelago 1
Malay Peninsula 1, 6, 7, 10, 25, 26, 30, 78
Malayu 8, 9
Manawgon 45
Manipur 14, 15
Manitasena 75
Mañjughoṣa 9

Mañjukumāra 53
Mañjuśrī 9, 40ff., 91
Mañjuśrīmūlakalpa 73
Mantrayāna 13, 78, 81, 98
Manuha 2, 97
Marco Polo 25
Markkaman 29
Marshall 90
Masud 75
Mauuggan 3
Maung Tin 64
Maynāmati 94
Menarn 24, 83
Mĕndut 10
Metriya 43
Mettañ 42
Metteya 42
Minhāj 75, 76
Mingalazedi 58
Minnanthu 51, 56
Mleccha 75
Mo-chia-man 29
Moens 13
Mo-ho-hsin 28
Mo-lo-yu 28, 29
Mrammadesa 2
Mṛtyuuañcana 36
Mṛtyuvañcanopa-deśatārāsādhana 38
Mṛtyuvañcana-sitatārāsādhana 38
Muhammad-i-Bakhtyar 75, 76, 77
Muner 76
Munśmatālaṁkāra 76
Muñjan 76, 77, 81, 85
Myingyan 68
Myinpagan 2, 49, 56, 57, 58
Myothit 45

N

Nāga 63, 70
Nāgarakrĕtāgama 13, 25, 26, 29
Nāgarī 12, 15, 22, 31, 32, 33, 34, 45, 46, 78, 82, 88, 89
Nāgārjuna 74
Nāgārjunīkoṇḍa 4, 74
Nāgasena 7
Nagayon 58
Nālagiri 55
Nālandā 10, 33, 46, 74, 93
Nāmasaṅgīti 53
Nandamañña 16, 51ff., 91, 92, 98, 99
Nandī 57
Naṅgata 77, 80
N'an hai chi kuli nai fa ch'en 23
Narapatisithu 54
Narathu 93
Nateśvara 77
Nathlaung 82
Nausari 75
Negapatam 10
Nepal 10, 13, 14, 37, 46, 51, 70, 76, 93
Nikobar 27, 78
Nirvāṇa 42
Nizām-ud-din 76
Nyaung Sawrahan 63
Nyaung-u 50
Nyāyabindu 36
Nyāyabindu-ṭīkā 36

O

Odantapurī 75, 76, 81, 82
Odantavihāra 76
Oḍiviṣa 74, 76
Odraviṣaya 74
Orissa 85

P

Padmapāṇī 9
Pagan 2 ,4, 5, 14, 16, 17, 31, 32, 33, 34, 38, 40ff
Pagan Rājā Van Thit 43
Pag Sam Jon Zang 72, 95, 98
Pahtogyi 64
Pahtonge 64
Paigu 79, 85
Pajigu 85
Pakhoi 27
Pan 12
pañcamakāras 13
Paññasāmī 35
P'an-p'an 27
Panthagu 5
Pāla 13, 14, 76, 82, 95, 97
Pallava 4, 5, 6, 12, 88
Palembang 6, 24, 25, 28
Parhetanandaghoṣa 86
Pasuruan 29
Paṭaveṣa 74
Paṭaviṣaya 74
Pateikkara 93, ,94
Pathama-min-gaung 67
Paticcasamuppāda sutta 4
Paṭikārā 93, 94
Patothamya 58, 64
Paṭṭikera 94
Pawon 10
Paya-thon-zu 16, 51ff., 92, 98
Payigu 79
Payigudvipa 78, 79
Pegu 3, 24, 38, 72, 79, 80, 81, 85, 86, 89
Pelliot 6, 7, 23, 25, 26, 28, 34, 68
Pei shih 25
Pembuan 28
P'ĕn-p'ĕn 28
Phayre 23, 24, 62, 70, 93
Phiranga 86
P'iao 3
Pinya 34, 66, 68, 79
P'nen-gi 86
P'o-li 28
P'o-lu-shih 28
Popa 62
Potala 86
Potalaka 86
Prajñāpāramitā 46, 60
Prapañca 13
Prāsāt Prām Lovén 7
Pratibimba Stūpa 86
Pratītasena 77
P'ren gi 86
Prome 3, 5, 19, 43, 44, 88, 89, 96, 97
Ptolemy 15
Pugāmā 64, 77, 85
Pugarama 64
Pukam (Pukām) 74, 75, 77
Pukan (Pukāṇ) 75, 85
Pukhang 75
Pukham 76, 77, 80, 81
Pulakeśi Avanijanāśraya 75
Pundravardhana 85
Punna 64
Purī 85
Pyogingyi-kon 90
Pyu 3, 19, 20, 21, 80, 90, 96, 97

R

Rāḍha 74.
Rājendracola 25, 26, 74
Rājendravarman 11
Ra k'an 85
Rakhān 77, 80
Raktamālā 38
Raktayamārisādhana 38

Raktayamāritantrarāaja 38
Ramaññadesa 2
Rāmapāla 76
Rame Khombeng 63
Raṇavaṅkamalla 94
Rangoon 43, 58
Rathika (sena) 75, 76
Ratnabhānu 7
Ratnamālā 38
Ratnamālā-ṭīkā 38
Ratnamati 75
Ratnarakṣita 76
Ratnasambhava 46
Ratnasiṁha 7
Rattamālā 36, 38
Rattamālā-ṭīkā 36
Raverty 75, 76, 77
Raviśrībhadra 76, 81
Ray 34, 82, 91
Red Province 29
Rinchen bzaṅ-po 38
Rockhill 25
Rudradeva 32
Rouffaer 28

S

Sāthanamālā 42, 46
Saggaing 66, 79
Sahaja 94
Śailendra 9, 10, 11
Śākyamuni (Śākya) 2, 9
Śākyaśrī 76
Samaṇakuṭṭakas 16, 17, 62ff
Samataṭa 24, 49, 93
Sam-bha-laḥi-lam-yig 84
Saṁghadāsa 75
Sammiti-nikāya 8, 28, 29
Samuti 68
Sandhādvīpa 86
San-fo-ch'i 25
Sang-hyang Kamahāyānikan 13
Sans rgyas Sbas pa 84
Śāntinātha 36
Sāntipāda 86
Sārnāth 20, 33, 46
Sarvadvīpa 86
Sarvāstivāda 7, 8, 19ff., 33, 89, 69
Sāsanavaṁsa 2, 16, 35, 62, 68, 69, 85, 97
Sawrahan 64
Sawyun 66
Schiefner 73ff
Schlegel 25
Seinnyet Pagodas 50
Seittopahto 64.
Sena 73, 75, 78, 80, 82, 95
Shan 67
She-ho-po-ti 8, 23, 27, 29
Shih-li-c'ha-ta-lo 3, 23, 26, 29, 30
Shin-li-fo-shih 28
Shin Arahan 54, 55, 64, 65, 71
Shu-chuan 23.
Shwekugyi 42, 54, 58
Shwesandaw 58
Shwezigon 58.
Siam 1, 8, 23, 27
Śila 74.
Siṁhajaṭi 78
Siṁhala 28, 78, 79
Sindhu (deśa) 28, 29, 76
Singapur 28
Siṅgasari 13
Śiva 13, 57
Śivaism (Śaiva) 11, 12, 13, 14.
Smith 3
Soṇa 3, 77
Śrāvakas 76, 77, 79, 81
Śrijñāna 76, 81
Śrikṣetra 3, 23, 24, 26, 27, 28

Śrīpādukā 79
Śrivijaya 8, 9, 10, 11, 25, 28
Ssu Ch'uan 23
Sthavira-nikāya 5, 28, 29
Sthaviravāda 7, 96
Subhajāta 78
Sudaungpyi Monastery 44
Sugata 42
Sui shu 25, 26
Sukhāvatī Lokeśvara 42
Sukhotaya 63
Sumatra 6, 8, 9, 11, 12, 13, 14, 25, 28, 30, 78, 86
Sumlūlā 42
Sūrya 60
Sūryadvīpa 86
Sūryaprabhā 46
Suvaṇṇabhūmi 3, 77, 79
Suvarṇadvīpa 78, 79, 85
Suvarṇapura 10

T

Tabaqāt-i-Nasiri 75, 76, 77
Tagoung (Tagaung) 15, 64
Taika 75
T'ai p'ing huan yū chi 28
Tājika 75, 76
Takakusu 8, 9, 21, 23, 24, 28, 29, 30
Talaing 2, 14, 42, 50, 67, 79, 96, 97
Talang Tuwo 6, 7
Tambadvīpa 68
Tamluk 79
Tampavati 64
Tāmradvīpa 78, 79, 86
Tāmraliṅgam 78, 79
Tāmralipti 14, 27, 78, 79, 95
Tāmraparṇī 79
Tāmrapattanam 78, 79
Tanaṅsari 79
Tananśrī 79
Tangyur 36, 37
Tanjore 25, 78
Tan-mo-ling 78
Tan-mo-li-ti 78
Tao-lin 28, 78, 79
Tā Prohm 6, 7
Tan-tan 28
Tantra 12, 34
Tantrayāna 13, 14, 33, 98
Tārā 9, 40ff., 89, 92, 93
Tāranātha 33, 38, 39, 72ff., 82ff., 95, 97, 98
Ta-ta 28
Taung-dwin 34
Tavoy 26.
Taw Sein Ko 62, 70
Telegu 96
Tennasserim 24, 25, 26, 54, 71, 81, 86, 87, 98
Thai 63
Thaittang 64, 97.
Thamati (Thamahti) 62, 64, 65, 97
Thanbula 56, 58, 92
Thap-muōi 7
Thatbiññyu 54, 58
Thaton 2, 3, 5, 26, 32, 33, 64, 68, 79, 96, 97
Tharakittara (Thari) 3, 64.
Thaungdut 15
Theravāda 1, 2, 3, 4, 5, 8, 14, 15, 17, 22, 30, 32, 33, 38, 40, 43, 52, 65ff., 83, 86, 91, 94, 97, 98, 99
Thihathu 66
Thinlinpahto 64.
Thiripyissaya 64
Thūpārāma 79
Tibet 23, 76, 84
Tipperah 33, 77, 85, 93

Tipurā 85
Tīrtha 75, 76
Tirumalaya 74
Tnaṅsi 79
To-lo-po-ti 23, 24, 27
Tripurā 77, 85
Tripurā Rājamālā 94
Tucci 84
Tufan 23
Tugma 15
Tukhāra 73
Turks 77
Turuṣka 76, 78, 82
Twante 44

U

Udayana 74
Udyāna 73
Upakeśinī 46
Upanahasaṁwatirājawaṁsakathā 79
Uragapuram 4
Uttara 77
Uttarajīva 5, 94
Uzana 56

V

Vairocana 13, 46
Vajrācārya 61
Vajrapāṇi 9
Vajrāsana 75
Vajrasattva 40, 50, 51, 92
Vajraśrī 76
Vajrayāna 54, 60
Vandeye-śses-sde 36
Vaṅga 74
Vasubandhu 77, 80, 97
Vat Prey Vier 7
Vedasattha 35
Vedasatthakovida 35
Veṅgī 5
Vredenburg 92
Vibhaṅga 4
Vidyābhūṣaṇa 36
Vikramāṅkadeva-caritam 75
Vikramaśilā 75, 76, 82
Vimalaprabhā 37
Vinaya 21, 22, 78, 81
Vinītadeva 36
Vihār 76
Viṣṇu 7, 13
Vogel 6
Vraha Guhya 12

W

Watters 21, 79, 81
We-Lei 27
Wellesley Province 6
Winstedt 28

Y

Yamunā 57, 76
Yaśovarman 11
Yathepyi 64
Yavadvīpa 78
Yindaik-kwin 41, 91.
Yule 68

Z

Zegu Pagoda 90
Zigon 63.

Description of Plates

Fig. 1: Mañjuśrī. Bronze. Hmawza. For description, see p. 41. c. 7-8th cent. A.D. A wrong identification has been suggested in the text. Indeed, the figure on the crown is not Amitābha, but Akṣobhya, and hence the image must be one of Mañjuśri.

Mark the facial physiognomy, especially the curve of the lips, and the rather heavy modelling of the nose, which are all unlike what have up to now been found in Burma, but are not uncommon in old Cambodian art. It is not improbable that the image was bodily carried over from some place in the old Hindu colony of Kamboj.

Fig. 2: Avalokiteśvara and Maitreya flanking the Buddha. Bronze. Pagan. c. 11-12th cent. For description, see p. 45; for descriptions of similar representations of Avalokiteśvara and Maitreya flanking the Buddha, see pp. 43-45. Dr. N.J. Krom, relying on finds from Java, suggested to me that they may also represent Avalokiteśvara and Vajrapāṇi.

Note the *dharmacakra* flanked by two crouching gazelles which locates the scene at Sarnath, but the Buddha is depicted in *bhūmisparśa-mudrā* locating the scene at Bodh-gayā.

Fig. 3: Avalokiteśvara. Bronze. Pagan. c. 10-11th cent. For description, see p. 41.

Fig. 4: Tārā. Stone. Pagan. c. 10-11th cent. For description, see p. 46.

Slight *tribhaṅga* pose, fore-arms broken, feet mutilated. *kuṇḍala, keyūra, mekhalā*.

Fig. 5: Probably Maitreya. Bronze. Thiyipyitsaya. Pagan. c. 10-11th cent.

Seated in *lalitāsana;* right hand in *abhaya-mudrā,* left resting on a lotus; two *nāgakeśara* stems rise on two sides in delightful curves forming a frame as it were. The hair is done into a *mukuṭa* consisting of long and curly locks. The lower garment is fitted tight to the body while a sash diagonally passes round the upper part of the body.

Fig. 6: Lokanātha. Bronze. Pagan. c. 10-11th cent. For description, see p. 48.

Fig. 7: Lokanātha. Bronze. Pagan. c. 11-12th cent. For description, see p. 48.

For another recent find of what I consider to be a representation of Lokanātha, *see An. R.A.S.I.*, 1980-84, Part Two, pl. XCIX(c). Noteworthy is the writing in Nāgarī characters of about the 11-12th cent., recording the Buddhist formula.

Fig. 8: Bodhisattva, probably Maitreya. Wall-painting. Nandamañña temple, Minnanthu, Pagan. c. 13-14th cent.

Standing in slight *ābhaṅga*, richly ornamented : *mukuṭa, hāra, keyūra, valaya, mekhalā, nūpura,* printed or embroidered skirt. Right hand hanging and holding in delicate grasp a stalk of *nāgakeśara* flower, left hand in *abhaya-mudrā.*

Fig. 9: Bodhisattva, probably Maitreya. Wall-painting. A small temple. Pagan. c. 13-14th cent.

Standing in slight ābhaṅga; richly ornamented : *mukuṭa, hāra, valaya, keyūra, mekhalā, nūpura,* printed skirt. Right hand in *abhaya-mudrā,* left hand hanging and holding in delicate grasp a stalk of *nāgakeśara* flower.

Fig. 10: Bodhisattva. Wall-painting. Paya-thon-zu temple, Minnanthu, Pagan. c. 14th cent.

Standing on lotus pedestal. Ornaments : *mukuṭa, kuṇḍala, hāra, keyūra, valaya, mekhalā,* printed skirt. Hands in the attitude of making offerings, evidently to the Buddha in the sanctum.

Fig. 11: Bodhisattva. Wall-painting. Paya-thon-zu temple, Minnanthu, Pagan. c. 14th cent.

Standing in slight *tribhaṅga,* on lotus pedestal; halo round head; ornaments: *mukuṭa, hāra, keyūra, valaya, mekhalā,* printed skirt. Right band in *vyākhyāna-mudrā,* left hand doubled upwards to clasp a *nāgakeśara* stalk. Two Śaktis clinging on two legs.

Fig. 12: Bodhisattva, probably Avalokiteśvara. Wall-painting. Paya-thon-zu temple, Minnanthu, Pagan. c. 14th cent.

Standing in slight *ābhaṅga*; ten hands holding attributes that can hardly be recognised; of them two are, however, held before the chest in *dharmacakra-mudrā;* ornaments : *mukuṭa, hāra, keyūra, valaya, mekhalā, mūpura,* printed skirt. Two female figures, probably Śaktis, seated with folded hands on two sides.

Fig. 13: Bodhisattva with Śaktis. Wall-painting. Paya-thon-zu temple, Minnanthu, Pagan. c. 14th cent.

Standing in *tribhaṅga* with two Śaktis clinging on two sides; richly ornamented as usual; also see photonegatives of the Archaeological Survey of Burma, Nos. 64/3211 of 1929-30, 58/3205 of 1929-30, 59/3206 of 1929-30, and 66/3213 of 1929-30.

Fig. 14: Bodhisattva, perhaps Mahārājalilā Mañjuśrī or Lokanātha. Wall-painting. Nandamañña temple, Minnanthu, Pagan. c. 14th cent. For description, see pp. 55-56.

Note the winged *gandharva* in front who is seated on the point of the trunk of the *makara,* depicted below (not reproduced) as in the tradition of the Eastern School of Art of Bengal and Bihar, to be seen on both sides of the main figure.

Fig. 15: Bodhisattva and Śakti in embrace. Wall-painting, Nandamañña temple, Minnanthu, Pagan, c. 14th cent. Both standing in slight *ābhaṅga* and with aureoles.

Bodhisattva on right embracing Śakti with left hand, and Śakti on left embracing Bodhisattva with right hand. Right hand of Bodhisattva is raised upwards while the left of Śakti is placed on the stretched-out arm of Bodhisattva. Both figures are richly ornamented and wear printed skirts. A haloed figure stands on the right of Bodhisattva.

Fig. 16: Wall-painting (outline copy) on the western portion of the south wall of the Abeyadana temple, Myinpagan, Pagan. c. 11th cent. For description, see pp. 59-60 ; see also *An. R.A.S.I.*, 1930-34, pp. 181-82.

Upper panel : on the right side of the empty niche is an ornamented and crowned figure standing in slight *ābbaṅga,* and holding a ring in the right hand and what seems to be more like a dagger than a sword in the left. On the left side is a similar figure holding a trident in the right and a ring in the left hand. They are probably simply *dvārapālas.*

The middle band shows six scenes which are difficult to identify. They seem to allude to some stories, and some of them are supposed to be Tāntrik in character.

Lower panel : the two upper figures seated in *ardhaparyaṅ kāsana* are undoubtedly Avalokiteśvara and Mañjuśrī respectively. The two figures seated below may tentatively be identified as Skanda or Kārtikeya and Sūrya respectively. The former holds a shield in the right and what seems to be a trident in the left. The latter holds a *cakra* in the right and a sword in the left. Both wear what seems to be felt boots. For the representations of another divinity with felt boots, see *An. R.A.S.I.*, 1930-34, pl. CI(a); this also comes from the Same Abeyadana temple.

Fig. 17: Lokanātha. Wall-painting. Abeyadana temple, Myinpagan, Pagan. c. 11th cent. F'or description, see p. 59.

Fig. 18: Hayagrīva. Wall-painting. Abeyadana temple, Myinpagan, Pagan. c. 11th cent. For description, see pp. 60-61.

Fig. 19: Śakti. Wall-painting (outline copy). Abeyadana temple, Myinpagan, Pagan. c. 11th cent.

Goddess seated in *padmāsana* on lotus seat; six bands, two on two sides in *varada-mudrā,* one on the right in *tarjanīmudrā,* others in *mantra-mudrā.* Ornaments : *mukuṭa,* hāra, keyūra, valaya, mekhalā, kuṇḍala, and printed skirt.

Fig. 20: Probably Tārā. Wall-painting (outline copy). Abeyadana temple, Myiopagan, Pagan. c. 11th cent.

Goddess seated on a lotus seat in *lolitāsana,* two hands as if in prayer; to the right rises a stalk with lotus in half bloom; jewels and ornaments, printed bodice and skirt.

Fig. 21: Lokanātha. Wall-painting (outline copy). Abeyadana temple, Myinpagan, Pagan. c. 11th cent.

Crowned and aureoled divinity seated in *lalitāsana* on a lotus seat. Right hand in *varada* and left in *abhayamudrā;* to the left rises a lotus stalk; usual ornaments; flanked by two aureoled and ornamented divinities.

Fig. 22: Śiva riding the bull Nandī. Wall-painting. Abeyadana temple, Myinpagan, Pagan. c. 11th cent. For description, see p. 57, f.n. 3.

Fig. 23: Yamunā riding her *vāhana* the tortoise. Wall-painting, Abeyadana temple, Myiopagan, Pagan, c. 11th cent. For description, see p. 57, f.n. 3.

Fig. 24: Probably Viṣṇu riding his *vāhana* Garuḍa. Wall-painting (outline copy). Abeyadana temple, Myinpagan, Pagan. c. 11th cent.

Viṣṇu kneeling, with hands folded probably in adoration to the Buddha in the sanctum. Note the Garuḍa holding a pair of snakes in his toes and carrying the *kumbha* in his hands ; note also the *pāśa* in one of the left hands of Viṣṇu and an indistinct object in one of his right.

Fig. 25: Three-headed Brahmā riding his *vāhana,* the haṁsa. Wall-painting (outline copy). Abeyadana temple, Myinpagan, Pagan. c. 11th cent.

Fig. 26: Śiva. Wall-painting. Abeyadana temple, Myinpagan, Pagan. c. 11th cent. For description, see p. 60, where I suggested a wrong identification. The attributes of Śiva, *viz., the jaṭā-nukuṭa, the akṣamālā,* and the trident are too clear to be missed.

For other Brahmanical representations in the Abeyadana, see *An. R.A.S.I.,* 1930-34, p. 183.

For description of some of the mural paintings in the Abeyadana and Kubyaukki temples, Myinpagan, Pagan, representing gods and goddesses of Sanskrit Buddhism and also of Brahmanism, see *An.R.A.S.I.*, 1930-34, pp. 181-84.

Fig. : 1

Fig. : 2

Fig. : 3

Fig. : 4

Fig. : 5

Fig. : 6

Fig. : 7

Fig. : 8

Fig. : 9

Fig. : 10

Fig. : 11

Fig. : 12

Fig. : 13

Fig. : 14

Fig. : 15

Fig. : 16

Fig. : 17

Fig. : 18

Fig. : 19

Fig. : 20

Fig. : 21

Fig. : 22

Fig. : 23

Fig. : 24

Fig. : 25

Fig. : 26